POOLE AFTER WORLD WAR II
1945–1953

POOLE AFTER WORLD WAR II

1945-1953

By John Hillier

POOLE HISTORICAL TRUST

This volume is published by the Poole Historical Trust whose primary aims are the promotion of research into and the publication of works on the history and life of Poole and the surrounding areas.

Previous publications

Pride of Poole
An Album of Old Poole
Mansions & Merchants of Poole & Dorset
Brownsea Islander
Poole & World War II
Portfolio of Old Poole
Ebb-Tide at Poole
History of the Town of Poole, 1839 (reprint)
Art in Poole & Dorset
Victorian Poole

ISBN 1 873535 00 7

The index by Brian J Galpin
Designed by Keith Godwin
Photography & photographic copying by Stephen Courtney
Printed and bound by Latimer Trend & Company Ltd, Plymouth

ACKNOWLEDGEMENTS

I am grateful for the loan of documents and for help in research to the Poole Corporation and its Museum Service, and to my fellow trustees, Ian Andrews, Brian Elliott, Brian Galpin and Graham Smith in the production of this volume.

Photographic film, like many other commodities, was not freely available in the years covered by this book. I am therefore very indebted to Laxton Blinkhorn, who took most of the portraits of members of the Council; to the Borough of Poole Museum Service photographic collection; to Mrs C W Douie for the use of Miss Llewellin's scrapbook; to the Poole Corporation for photographs from the Poole Guides; to the Poole Herald; to Mr H A Carter for the photograph of Herbert Carter and to Miss Annette Bailey and Mr D R Davis, as well as many others, for the use of photographs.

CONTENTS

In September, 1945, the first men to be released from Japanese prison camps arrived in Poole, and were welcomed by the Mayor, Mervyn Wheatley, and a cheering crowd at Poole Quay.

PREFACE

IN 1945, at the end of World War II, there was much to do to return the town to peacetime conditions. Scores of Air Raid shelters and static water tanks littered the streets, five thousand of the town's houses had been war-damaged and needed repair. All the beaches had been mined and covered with tubular fortifications and barbed-wire; a great arc of 'dragons' teeth had been constructed round the 'Poole Redoubt' and the rail and road approaches had been protected by concrete 'pill boxes' to house the defending forces.

The war and the earlier preparations for war had meant that no houses or schools had been built for seven years. Industry had been turned over to war production. Even before hostilities ceased, men and women were being laid off as war production was cut back. Eight thousand Poole men and women, then serving in the armed forces, would need jobs on their demobilisation, as would the hundreds then employed in the Civil Defence forces.

In addition to Poole's industry changing to peacetime production and Poole Council providing housing and schooling for its swollen population, there were other urgent problems needing action. Over 700 of its existing houses in the Old Town had been condemned as slums prior to the war and were still in use. The rapid increase in population prior to the war had left many miles of its roads, unmade-up, gravelled builders' roads, without street lighting or drainage. Its streets were inadequately lit by gas lamps, and the town was in desperate need of an extension and modernisation of its sewage system. In addition there was the town's old ambition to become in charge of its own destiny by becoming a County Borough, and to have the great area of the borough, then with a 'Bournemouth' postmark, changed to 'Poole'.

The following pages chronicle the early struggles, frustrations and successes, of the townspeople and their Council, in their efforts to rectify these shortcomings and to fulfil their ambitions for the town.

Top: Tubular scaffolding stretched along the length of Poole Bay.

Bottom: 'Dragons' Teeth' behind Wimborne Road.

1945

WHO GOES HOME?

'An Apology . . . our sea-front bore
a mass of defence works . . . and the
work of clearance was a task of
some magnitude . . .
When therefore you visit us,
remember that such scars as you
may see are a part of the price
we willingly paid to remain a
free country, and so to welcome once
again our many friends from home
and abroad . . .'

(*Poole Guide, 1947*)

Poole ceased to feel itself in the front line of the war in July, 1944, when the naval base at Cherbourg and the rocket launching sites being prepared in the peninsula had been overrun by the Allied Armies. Then, a month later, when the Allies reached the German border, the war seemed as good as over, and it was possible to think of peace.

The Council knew that it would be an enormous task to put the town back to its peace-time condition. The town had been transformed into a veritable fortress, entry into it barred to all but its own residents and approved visitors. The Quay, the beaches and the whole of the Sandbanks peninsula had been forbidden even to Poole townspeople, except those residents of Sandbanks who were allowed through the barricade at Banks Road on the production of a pass, signed by the Town Clerk. The Quay was fenced off and guarded by American GIs, and long lines of tubular scaffolding and barbed wire stretched along the beaches. The harbour itself was a 'no-go' area, taken over by the Admiralty and the British Overseas Aircraft Corporation, and guarded by guns of the Royal Artillery stationed on Brownsea Island and at points along the coast; a minefield was laid off Brownsea, and two old naval ships stood ready in the harbour to be sunk to block the Main Channel if all else failed. To landward, the quays and main railway lines were guarded by pill boxes and a wide arc of large concrete blocks, known as 'Dragons' Teeth', and, on the south western approaches to the town, a deep moat had been dug to act as a tank trap.

The town itself was cluttered with the impedimenta of war, much of it caused by the Council itself. It had built Air Raid shelters and placed large 'Static Water Tanks' at all strategic places of the borough, and it had turned over those parts of the parks and recreation grounds not taken by the military, to provide thousands of allotments to meet the demand induced by the Government's 'Dig for Victory' campaigns.

By this time the Royal Marines, the Royal Navy support ships, and the units of the American invasion Sub-Base had left their camp on Ham Common; their 68 temporary buildings, spread over the 100 acres of the land, were empty and deserted, as was the 'hard' at Lake Road, first used by the RAF's Sunderland squadrons. All that was left of the invasion force were the 60 Coast Guard vessels of No 1 Rescue Flotilla and a part of the US Navy at the Quay. American GIs were no longer seen in the town and many of the original thousand US Coastguardsmen had left. The lady Commandant of the American Red Cross had thanked the Mayor for the use of the Guildhall (which she referred to as 'the ancient monument') which had been used to provide showers and a canteen for the American troops and, by the autumn of 1944, the Old Town had already seemed suddenly quiet and empty.

It was not too early to begin putting the town into some sort of shape, the Council decided. The static water tanks were emptied, and a start was made to collect the Morrison shelters which had been loaned to householders, and the Council gave notice to quit to the holders of allotments in the more sensitive areas of the borough, such as Parkstone Park and the tennis courts at Poole Park. It closed the Air Raid shelters and released some of the staff, such as the Shelter Superintendent, the Canteen Services Organiser and 132 of the Civil Defence personnel. By December it was thought possible to stand down the Home Guard and Lt/Col Alderman Wheatley, o/c of the Poole 3rd Battalion of the Dorset Home Guard, held its final parade, and all seemed set for a gradual transition to peace.

But the progress of the war did not go according to plan. In the same month as the Home Guard was disbanded, everything was put on 'hold' as the German Panzers counter-attacked the Allied Armies and drove a deep wedge between the British and the American Armies and the bitter 'Battle of the Bulge' ensued which put paid to further anticipation of peace, as it was obvious that the war was not, after all, going to be ended that year.

There was, though, no reason to defer making plans for peace. One of the great problems was clearly going to be that of housing. No houses had been

Top: The US No 1 Rescue Flotilla at Poole Quay.

Bottom: The first Poole Grammar School.

built for over seven years and over 400,000 of the country's houses had been destroyed by enemy action and very many more had been damaged. Poole's housing situation was clearly going to be as bad as anywhere in England. 82 of its houses had been completely destroyed and 5,000, nearly a quarter of the town's total stock of housing, were war-damaged. What was more, nearly all the 762 of its houses, mainly in the Old Town, having been condemned as being unfit for human habitation in 1937, were still occupied. The Council decided that the town required at least a further 4,000 new houses for its population to be adequately housed. It began to plan where the first of these houses could be built.

Another serious problem of peace which was going to face Poole was the lack of school accommodation. Between 1931 and the outbreak of war, Poole's population had risen by nearly 10,000. It had been such a rapid increase that its Education Committee had been unable to provide sufficient school accommodation and this had meant that the town had too few schools when war started. Even during the war the Education Committee had only been able to accommodate the children by taking over other premises, mainly church halls, to provide extra classrooms and, when Southampton's King Edward VI School had been evacuated to Poole at the outbreak of war, its pupils had to share the Poole Grammar School with the Poole pupils by putting both schools on half-time attendance.

The Education Committee began making its plans for peacetime. A new secondary school, it decided, was a first priority and, it calculated, a further five schools would be needed to meet demand. Like the Estates Committee in the case of housing, the Education Committee began considering in which localities its new schools could best be built.

There was, too, another obvious problem which was going to arise at the end of the war. It was hard to envisage then how the thousands of Poole men and women who were in war work and in the Civil Defence Services would be absorbed into peacetime employment, to say nothing of the estimated 8,000 Poole men and women of Poole who were serving in the Armed Forces.

To prepare for this eventuality, the Council, in January, 1945, appointed a special 'Industrial Advisory Committee' comprising Col H C Wallis of Wallis Tin Stamping, Mr F W Crawshaw of the South Western Pottery, Mr Reg Tarrant of the Dorset Iron Foundry and seven other local businessmen. Its duties were to help industries adapt to peacetime conditions, and to advise the Council on how new industries could best be attracted to the town.

In addition to these problems which would, in one form or another, affect the whole country, there were Poole's individual problems which had been put in abeyance by the war. The most important of these was that of the drainage of the town. Large areas of the town, including Merley, Bearwood, Canford Magna and Waterloo to the north of the borough, and the western half of Hamworthy to the south, were unsewered. Some 2,500 people already lived in these areas, their drainage served by nearly 1,000 cesspools and pail closets. Moreover, the Broadstone sewage works, built by the old Poole Rural District Council in 1922, was overloaded and obsolescent, and the works which dealt with the eastern half of Hamworthy could not cope with further connections.

Prior to the war, the three boroughs of Poole, Bournemouth and Christchurch had formed a Joint Sewerage Committee which had agreed a scheme to deal with the sewage of the three towns, the bulk of which was then being discharged into Poole Bay through nine separate outfalls. The scheme tentatively agreed by the three boroughs before the war was that the sewage of the three towns should, after some treatment, be discharged through a single outfall running out to sea from a point near Hengistbury Head.

At the end of 1944 the Poole Council felt it was not too early for the Joint Committee to be re-constituted so that the scheme could be revived, formally adopted, and plans could be made to implement it. It therefore asked the Bournemouth Council to agree to the re-appointment of the Joint Committee. The Bournemouth Council agreed but, when the Joint Committee met early in 1945 it was already clear that the Bournemouth Council had lost all enthusiasm for the joint scheme and that it was not easily going to be revived.

There was, however, an atmosphere of ready co-operation between the Councils in considering what should be done to prepare plans for the future development of the towns. In those days, when there was no threat to their individual integrity, the Councils of Poole and Christchurch were only too ready to take part in joint committees with the Bournemouth Council, and a Joint Planning Advisory Committee of the three Councils was formed in 1944. What was more, the Committee acted with unusual decisiveness. At its second meeting in January, 1945, it agreed that the best way forward would be to appoint an independent expert planner to prepare a Development Plan for the three towns.

The leading expert of the day was Sir Patrick Abercrombie, Professor of Town Planning at London University. He had already prepared development plans for Dublin, London and many other towns. It was agreed that he should be appointed with the Bournemouth Council paying 60% of the costs, Poole 30% and Christchurch 10%.

But the Council did not consider that this agreement in any way inhibited it in deciding on urgent domestic matters and, in the same month that Sir Patrick was appointed, it was resolved that: '*The Council, being of the opinion that the High Street is narrow and inconvenient, and that it is desirable that such street be widened, an improvement line of 60 feet should be made, to which such street should be widened.*'

A month or so later, the Council followed this resolution by making a similar improvement line for the Quay. At times during the war the Quay had been desperately congested. The Council decided that it needed considerable widening if it was to meet the likely demands of peace and it made an improvement line to bring the Quay up to a consistent width of 86 feet as measured from the Quay wall.

These decisions were well received by the public and Press, but one or two Councillors had misgivings, especially about the proposed widening of the Quay. A month or so later, Alderman Shortt, seconded by Councillor Mrs MacAndrew, put a motion before the Council, asking it to agree: *'That in all schemes for the improvement of the thoroughfare in the neighbourhood of the Quay, it will be the policy of the Council not to interfere (where possible) with the ancient buildings and, in particular, with the blocks of buildings known as the Custom House and the Harbour Office.'*

But the Council was in no mood to allow the reconstruction of Poole to be impeded by such niceties, and it rejected the motion.

Meanwhile, in November, 1944, the Council had re-elected Alderman 'Joe' Bright as its Mayor for a record seventh consecutive year. He was a short, roly-poly sort of man with noticeably short arms, but was also a determined, but amiable man, who seemed only irritated when called 'Joe', – as everybody seemed to do! He had come from Wimborne as a master baker to establish his bakery behind a small shop which he opened in High Street and from which he did a most considerable trade.

But it was the old Council stalwart, Councillor Willie Stickland, who, in 1907 had founded a wholesale confectionery and tobacco business at Beech House in Wimborne Road, and who had been Mayor in 1937 and re-elected Deputy Mayor to Alderman Bright, who enunciated the main peacetime aims of the Poole Council. He did so at the annual meeting of the Society of Poole Men in April, 1945, on being elected the Society's President, when he said: *'I want to see Poole obtain its status as the Town and County of Poole, separate from the County of Dorset, with the Post Office and Postmaster of its own, and Branksome Park, Canford Cliffs and Sandbanks, some of the best parts of Poole, with a Poole postmark, and not Bournemouth-Poole.'*

By this time the end of the war was certain enough for the Civil Defence services to be disbanded and, on 2 May, 1945, the final act was taken by the closure of the Headquarters' Control Centre. The last entry in its log book read: *'Report Centre locked up. Telephone Exchange, Bournemouth Report Centre and Naval Officer in charge, and all concerned notified. Who goes home?'*

The following day the war in Europe was officially ended and Poole and the rest of the country could at last celebrate, and the Council could restart its efforts to put Poole on a peaceful footing.

That same month, by coincidence, the Labour Party, had arranged its Annual Conference in Bournemouth and, though war was still being waged in the Far

Top: FW Crawshaw, Managing Director of the South Western Pottery.

Bottom: Alderman Joseph Bright, Mayor.

Bottom right: Cartoon drawing of Councillor 'Willie' Stickland prior to the war.

Top: Major JJ Llewellin, MP.

Bottom: Alderman Mervyn Wheatley, MP.

East, one of its first decisions was to withdraw its support of Churchill's Coalition Government. Major Attlee promptly returned to London to inform Churchill of the decision, a decision which Churchill had no option but to accept, even though he strongly felt that a General Election should await the end of the war in the Far East. He resigned, asked the King to dissolve Parliament, formed a Caretaker Government and called a General Election.

Poole was then part of the East Dorset Parliamentary constituency, which also included Swanage and Wimborne and their surrounding rural areas. The sitting Conservative member, Hall Caine, had already indicated that he would not stand for re-election. However, the local Conservative Party felt confident of success in that it believed that Major J J Llewellin of Upton House, a man well known and respected in the area and who had held various posts in the Coalition Government, would agree to stand as its candidate.

Their assumption, however, was not followed up by an early formal invitation and, before this had been done, they heard that Major Llewellin had accepted an invitation to stand for the Uxbridge Constituency, and the local Conservatives were left with no candidate. After some urgent meetings, they found a likely candidate in Alderman Major Mervyn Wheatley, the Chairman of the Poole Finance Committee and, lately, the Officer Commanding the 3rd Battalion of the Dorset Home Guard.

No one could be confident about the outcome of that election. The last General Election had been held in 1937, and the 1945 election was to be held on a Register of Electors which was some eight years old. Mervyn Wheatley was also well known locally, but was not young and must have been considered as somewhat of a stand-in candidate. The Labour Party had a strong candidate in Lieutenant Commander Fletcher-Cooke, who was well thought of and supported by the hierarchy of the Labour Party. The Liberal candidate, Lieut/Col Mander, could rely on a loyal core of supporters in East Dorset.

The election was held on 5 July, 1945, but, with the result having to await the arrival of the votes of the men and women serving in the Forces overseas, it could not be declared until the 26th July.

Alderman Wheatley had narrowly won. The result was:

Lt/Col M J Wheatley (Con)	26,561
Lt/Cdr C Fletcher-Cooke (Lab)	25,093
Lt/Col J A H Mander (Lib)	8,975

The success of Colonel Wheatley was only mildly surprising, but the results nationwide, giving a majority of 146 seats to Labour and with Clement Attlee supplanting Churchill as Prime Minister, surprised many people at home, and even more abroad.

Mr Attlee and his Government were not called on to be responsible for the prosecution of the war for long for, less than a month afterwards, on 23rd August, following the dropping of an atomic bomb on Hiroshima and Nagasaki, the Japanese surrendered.

Within days of this, however, President Truman had cancelled Lend-Lease Aid on which Britain had relied for the past three years and, suddenly, Britain found itself at peace, but in a serious financial position. The Government was faced with the daunting task of making good the ravages of war as well of converting the war-time economy to the needs of peace, but had little money to do either.

The Treasury reported the dire facts to the new Cabinet. It was told that it was no 'Brave New World' which the Cabinet faced, but a 'Cruel Real World'. Lord Keynes, the Government's economic adviser, said that the Country had indulged in 'unparalleled financial imprudence in the cause of humanity'. The country had ended the war with its merchant marine decimated, its overseas investments sold, and with debts of £3,500m against its meagre £500m reserves.

Lord Keynes was despatched to America to try to negotiate a huge loan. He did not find it easy but, eventually, after three months' of difficult negotiations, a loan of $3.75 billion was raised but, even then, only at the expense of accepting harsh conditions. But, at least, the country had a breathing space to try to put itself to rights.

Top: Councillor Geoffrey Bravery.

Bottom: Wilson Kenyon, Town Clerk.

1946

MARKS OF GRATITUDE

'Mr Churchill should be admitted to the Honorary roll of Freedom of the Borough as a mark of gratitude . . .'

(*Council resolution, March, 1946*)

The Council decided that the first year of peace was not too early for it to begin its efforts to gain a 'Poole' postmark for all the areas of the town. With the help of the town's new Member of Parliament, the Council's ex-Chairman of the Finance Committee, the Council obtained an interview with the Postmaster General, and it appointed Councillors Bravery and Alderman Bright and the Town Clerk William Kenyon, to put its case.

However, as the three of them returned to Poole that evening they felt that they had made little impression on the Postmaster General and his officials, and that, even the achievement of this smaller of the town's ambitions, was not going to be easy.

The deputation's fears were soon confirmed. The Postmaster General wrote soon afterwards. He and his officers had considered what had been said, he wrote but there was no possibility of the Poole Head Office being enlarged to enable it to deliver letters to all parts of the town. It might, though, be possible for those parts of the Borough with a Bournemouth address to be given a 'Parkstone' address, at some time, but this would entail a future enlargement of the Parkstone Post Office to accommodate at least fifteen extra postmen.

But, though the town's ambition for an early 'Poole' postmark for the borough had been thwarted, hope arose that year that the council might soon achieve its main ambition, that of becoming again the master in its own town for Parliament had passed the Local Government (Boundary Commission) Act under which a Commission was to be set up to visit all parts of the country to make recommendations on the amendment of local government boundaries and powers.

However, it had to be accepted that the auguries for the Government to give the Council extra powers did not seem very favourable for the Education Act,

1944 was brought into operation that year whereby the responsibility for education in Poole was transferred to the Dorset County Council.

It was little comfort to the Poole Council that an earlier Poole Council in 1880 had not opted to become a County Borough, which had left the town in the category of a 'Non-County Borough' with hundreds of small towns (such as, locally, Wareham and Blandford with populations around 4,000 and rateable values under £250,000) whose populations and resources were insufficient to take on the responsibilities as an education authority. Nor did it greatly soothe the Council's lost dignity when the County Council immediately asked the Council's Education Committee to continue to be responsible for education matters, or that it later formally delegated most of these duties back to the town's Education Committee.

The Education Committee had already set out its plans which, happily, included the provision of a new secondary school, for the new Education Act also increased the school leaving age to 15, adding 860 to the school roll. Other provisions of the Act gave the Education Committee the responsibility to provide school meals and free milk as well as to provide nursery classes for children between 2 and 5 years old.

At least the Education Committee was able to provide early nursery classes by taking over the three wartime nurseries of the Council's Maternity & Child Welfare Committee but, for the rest of its new duties, the only short term solution was the erection of temporary classrooms and kitchens at existing schools.

But, although the Education Committee was generally given a free hand by the County Council, the dual responsibility did give rise to problems. The County reserved the duty to acquire school sites, and the Poole Committee, certain that the County had assured them of the early acquisition of the school site at Sylvan Road, entered into a building contract for the school not knowing that negotiations to buy the site had broken down, and that its acquisition had to await the completion of the prolonged process of the confirmation of a compulsory purchase order. There was, too, an early incident to remind the Education Committee that it was no longer its own master when the County Committee refused to rescind its resolution 'not to employ during the war any teacher who is exempt from military service', even though it would appear that the resolution had already been negated by the ending of the war!

Nor was the Council's loss of its ultimate authority for education the last blow to the Council's dignity in 1946. The Council had always believed that the Government's undertaking to return the fire brigade service to local government when the National Fire Service was disbanded meant that they would be returned to the Councils from which they had been taken. However, the Government felt itself under no such obligation. It decided that, so long as fire brigades were returned to local government, it had complied with its undertaking, and that, as most non-county boroughs were too small to operate their own fire brigades, the Government gave the responsibility to county boroughs and county councils. Then, to add to the Council's chagrin, the County Council decided to make the Headquarters of the new County Brigade at Weymouth, rather than at Poole, the largest brigade prior to war.

Meanwhile, the Council put a great deal of effort into providing new housing accommodation. This duty was primarily that of its Estates Committee. Soon after the ending of the war Alderman Bacon, the managing director of the ironmongers in High Street, had resigned after eighteen years' service, and Councillor Geoffrey Bravery, who had succeeded to his uncle's cinemas, two of which were in High Street, was elected Chairman.

The officer responsible for all the practical work of achieving the building and conversion of property was then John Barron, a Yorkshireman, known as the 'Borough Engineer', but who was not only the Council's engineer, but its architect, planning officer and parks manager. It was he who was responsible for the design of houses, preparation of sites, the building of roads and laying of sewers as well as the supervision of building contracts. The Town Clerk, Wilson Kenyon, another Yorkshireman, and Poole's first non-native town clerk, had the problem of negotiating the purchase and assembly of the land for the housing estates and obtaining Ministerial approvals and the preparation of building contracts.

The Government did what it could to help the Council provide extra housing accommodation. The War Office was instructed to transfer to the Council the requisition of houses which it had taken in the war. The Council was also empowered to requisition any empty house in the town unless the owner could satisfy the Council that he wished soon to occupy it himself. The Government also took powers to control the selling price of houses which it did by enacting that the maximum price of houses was to be 50% over their pre-war price. Local authorities, too were encouraged to enter into contracts with local builders to erect houses for the Council on housing plots owned by them at agreed prices and, a little later, Councils were authorised to grant licences for the erection of private houses, at specified selling prices, at the rate of one licence for a private house for every four houses built by the Corporation.

The Government, too, had ordered some 200,000 prefabricated bungalows, of which Poole had been allocated 200 and it also facilitated the sanction to borrow money from the Public Works Loan Board (at 2% interest) for the purchase of land and, so long as costs came within its prescribed limits, gave ready approval to building contracts.

But, although the Corporation was producing additional housing accommodation at a rate which compared very favourably with other towns, and was always

Top: John Barron, Borough Engineer.

Bottom: Poole Fire Brigade prior to the War.

slightly ahead of Bournemouth, the Committee was never satisfied with progress. As the dates for completion of building contracts continued to slip, often by many months, and the confirmation of compulsory purchase orders always took longer than the Committee felt reasonable, the Committee regularly mounted deputations to the Ministry, asking for more powers to tackle the problem or urging more Government action to raise production of building materials to reduce the frustrating delays in delivery and, in the end, persuaded the Ministry to allow them to borrow enough money to set up their own 'Works Department' to undertake the building and repair of Council houses.

But the provision of new housing, though still the primary responsibility of the Estates Committee, affected other Committees of the Council, especially in the provision of sewers and water supplies for the new estates.

Happily, sufficient land was found for early housing requirements in areas of the borough which were already sewered and, to deal with the rest of the borough, the Corporation entered into negotiations with the neighbouring local authorities to agree joint schemes. The Corporation planned a new sewage works at Turlin Moor, Hamworthy, to deal with the drainage of Hamworthy and Upton, and negotiations were entered into with Wimborne to agree a scheme to deal with the Canford and Merley areas in conjunction with Wimborne and Wimborne & Cranborne Councils at a new works in Wimborne.

Water supplies were no immediate problem. The Corporation's Water Department already supplied the borough (apart from part of Branksome Park and Canford Magna) and, though its works at Corfe Mullen, already supplying 870 million gallons of water each year, was nearing its capacity, it was not thought that there would be much difficulty in obtaining Ministry approval to a loan to provide additional supplies, especially as the Ministry was already pressing the Council to increase its area of supply so that areas of Dorset to the west of Poole could be provided with a piped water supply.

It was the Health Committee which was then responsible for the water undertaking, but it was not only in this capacity that it felt itself involved in the housing, sewerage and educational problems of the borough.

In his formal report of 1946 to the Ministry of Housing and Local Government, for instance, George Chesney, a large Ulsterman, Poole's Medical Officer of Health, who had done so much to track down the source of the local typhoid epidemic in 1936, reported that *'the housing shortage presents a health problem of magnitude and urgency'* which had been made worse by *'the quite exceptional rate of development which has been a marked feature for the last ten years'*. In his report for the following year, Dr Chesney reported that *'although national policy demanded that demolition should be deferred, the 762 houses scheduled for demolition at the outbreak of war, were still occupied, and were so bad, and the plight of the families in them so desperate, that rehousing cannot be longer delayed without undue*

Top: Alderney Hospital today.

Bottom: BOAC was busy during 1946, bringing nearly 10,000 passengers into Poole.

detriment to their health'.

The Health Committee, meanwhile, with memories of the 1936 typhoid outbreak pestered the Ministry of Food to make the pasteurisation of milk compulsory. It argued that the Ministry was wrong in asserting that it would need an Act of Parliament; an order, it claimed, could be made under the Defence Regulations. But the Ministry refused to act, though, a year later, it did make an order to ensure that only pasteurised milk was to be used in the manufacture of ice cream.

The Committee also disapproved of the Ministry of Food's arrangements for the slaughter of animals. In 1946 it centralised the slaughtering of animals from an area of fifteen miles radius round Poole at the slaughterhouse at Bushell Mill, near Fleets, in Poole. The Committee felt that the accommodation was insufficient and not conducive to the proper examination of the animals by its Sanitary Inspectors. It felt that the slaughterhouse should be enlarged or, better still, a new, purpose-built abattoir should be built. The figures for 1946 seemed to support the Committee's contention. They showed that 13,923 animals were slaughtered, made up of

Cattle	Cows	Calves	Sheep	Pigs
2381	1746	3907	4695	1194

Of these animals, the inspectors had found that 11.6% of the animals slaughtered were affected with tuberculosis, and that no less than 141,269 lbs of meat had had to be condemned.

The Committee also riled at the unsatisfactory sewerage arrangements of the borough and the lack of decision of the Joint Sewerage Committee. It scoffed at the Ministry of Health's bacteriological survey undertaken prior to the war which had reported that 'there was no high level of impurity in the sea water'. It only needed the naked eye, Dr Chesney retorted, to refute it.

He also made sure that the Committee's views reached the Ministry of Health. In his annual report to the Ministry of Health, Dr Chesney wrote that the sandy beaches of Poole Bay formed 'a natural aquatic playground', yet had nine outfall sewers discharging the sewage of a quarter of a million people, untreated except for disintegration and a modicum of chlorination', into the Bay'. 'If these unwholesome discharges were eliminated or diverted for scientific treatment,' he added, 'Poole Bay would not only form the finest stretch of bathing beaches in England, but aesthetically the most acceptable and, hygienically, the most salubrious'.

In fact, Dr Chesney had a suspicion that it might be the polluted sea water which caused the spread of poliomyelitis of which there was only one case in the 221 admissions to the Corporation's Infectious Diseases Hospital at Alderney that year but, the following year, it developed into epidemic proportions when 15 people were admitted with the disease, of whom three died, and the admissions of Poliomyelitis cases increased to 30, with two deaths, the following year.

The Health Department carried out careful checks on the sea water as well as of the bathing pools of the town and one of the stories, emanating from that Department, was that a sample of water, thought to be from an hotel bathing pool was found to be so unsatisfactory that an immediate order was made to close the pool, only for it to be found that the sample tested was not that from the hotel bathing pool, but from the sea!

Nor was it only sea water with which the Committee was concerned. A monthly report was made to the Committee by the bacteriologist of the County Council, then housed in the Municipal Buildings, on the quality of the water provided by the Corporation's Water Department, all of which were, happily, always found to be 'Class I' (Highly satisfactory) on the Ministry of Health's classification.

The Health Department went further, however, in checking for fluorides in the water supplied by the Corporation, which was low at 0.3 parts per million gallons. A comparison was made with the water supplied from the private source at Canford School and that supplied to Wimborne.

The Canford supply contained 2.8 parts of fluorides, and Wimborne's supply contained 1.0. The condition of the teeth of the children being supplied from the different sources was checked. Four children who had been drinking the Canford water had no dental caries at all, but their teeth were mottled, one embarrassingly so. The Wimborne children were found to have, on average, 3.5 teeth decayed or missing, compared with an average of over 4 in Poole.

The Medical Officer, as a result of his investigations, suggested the addition of 23 lbs of sodium fluoride to each million gallons of water. It would cost little, he reported, but would be of benefit to the teeth of the people in Poole. It was, however, not a matter which could then be considered and, when it was, it gave rise to strong views about any 'tampering' with the water supply, and the Poole Council never did agree to add fluorides to its water supply.

Up to this time there had been little or no political controversy in the Council. During the war Councillor Reeves, the Labour leader, had been Chairman of the Air Raid Precautions Committee and Alderman Dacombe, a Liberal, had been Chairman of the Town Planning Committee, even though there was a Conservative majority in the Council.

That year there was a very good example of this when, under the provisions of the Bournemouth & Poole Electricity Act, 1934, the Corporations had an option to buy out the company which expired in August, 1947. The Council considered the question quite pragmatically. The members satisfied themselves that, as private companies paid out 50% of their gross profits in interest and dividend payments against 30% by local authority undertakings, it was no surprise to find that local authority undertakings charged less for electricity than that provided by private companies. The Council agreed that the option to buy out the local electricity company should be exercised 'as soon as possible'.

Events, however, moved quickly that year. First, the electricity company revived a pre-war proposal to build an electricity generating station on the mudlands of Holes Bay. With the prospect of new jobs for Poole and for a most substantial increase in the rateable value of the town, the Council was only too happy to approve the plan. With the proposal, and with it becoming clear that the Government would be proceeding with its nationalisation programme, the Council quietly forgot its resolution to buy out the company.

But it was inevitable that political differences would arise, sooner or later, in the Council, and they first arose from the most unlikely topic of the grant of the Freedom of the Borough.

At the end of the war the Council had agreed that the Freedom of the Borough should be offered to the Dorset Regiment. It had even agreed the citation for the grant as being: '*In token and in honour of the men and women of Poole in the fighting services and particularly in honour of those who have fallen in action.*'

It had, though, not called the necessary special meeting of the Council formally to adopt the resolution. Early in 1946, it was agreed that the formal meeting would be held in May.

Meanwhile, however, Mervyn Wheatley, Poole's MP, had written to the Town Clerk suggesting that the Freedom of the Borough should be granted to Winston Churchill in view of his many earlier connections with the town when his aunt, Lady Cornelia Wimborne, lived at Canford and later Merley House and his friend and cousin, Freddie Guest, was MP for Poole. The Committee enthusiastically adopted the suggestion. It resolved that: '*Mr Churchill should be admitted to the Honorary Freedom of the Borough as a mark of gratitude and in high appreciation of his courageous and inspiring leadership of the nation through the perilous years of the recent world war.*'

It was, however, on this resolution that political differences arose in the Council. The eleven Labour members of the Council opposed it, and it was only carried by 20 votes to 11.

However, the Finance Committee, perhaps with foreknowledge that the Labour members, having made a point, would not persist with its opposition at the formal meeting of the Council where a two-thirds majority was necessary, submitted its resolution to the special meeting of the Council. At this meeting, called on the same day as the resolution to grant the Freedom to the Dorset Regiment, it was, like the resolution about the Dorset Regiment passed unanimously.

The ceremony of the granting of the Freedom to the Dorsets was held in the early evening of 11th November that year. A bronze casket was provided to hold the parchment scroll and the presentation was made at a parade of a detachment of the Regiment in front of the cricket pavilion in Poole Park. But the presentation of the Freedom to Mr Churchill had to be held in abeyance. Mr Churchill, in accepting the Freedom, had replied that he was unable to agree an early date for receiving the honour.

For all the vicissitudes of the year, it ended with an announcement which was important to Poole. It was that the Common's Constituency Committee had completed its survey of Parliamentary constituencies, and that it would be reporting to Parliament early in 1947. This raised Poole's hopes of again becoming a separate parliamentary constituency. In the Victorian era the town had first lost one of its two MPs and then had been made to share its one member with Swanage, Wareham and Wimborne and their rural areas. Not content with this rebuff, the County Justices had voted that Wimborne should become the election town for the East Dorset Constituency, rather than Poole. But, in 1946, with its population estimated by the Registrar General to have reached 78,540, Poole had every hope of becoming again a separate constituency and Poole's Sheriff would again be the town's Returning Officer for a Poole which had again its own Member of Parliament.

Top: The cap badge of the Dorset Regiment.

Bottom: The Branksome Chine stream. The stream had virtually dried up in 1946. The Council's efforts after the war to resuscitate it failed.

Borough and County of the Town of Poole

1d.

POOLE'S CASE

Resistance to Annexation by Bournemouth

REASONS WHY THE BOROUGH AND COUNTY OF THE TOWN OF POOLE MUST NOT BE ANNEXED BY THE COUNTY BOROUGH OF BOURNEMOUTH

"Poole and Dorset Herald" Photo.

Published by the Poole United Resistance Committee, Guildhall, Poole. 'Phone : Poole 34

The pamphlet published by the Poole United Resistance Committee.

1947

THE BOURNEMOUTH 'GRAB'

'If Bournemouth were a wise neighbour she would realise the greatest benefit to herself and her neighbours would come not from amalgamation but co-operation.'

(Poole Herald, 1947)

All elections had been cancelled for the duration of the war. Most of the members of the Council who had not been called up for military service had, by 1947, served for ten years. Others had been co-opted on to the Council to fill vacancies and some of them were only anxious to return to their businesses. The war years had been a gruelling time for all of the thirty-six members for they had, between them, served on fourteen Council committees and thirty-two sub-committees. Six of them had also served as Harbour Commissioners, ten of them as Guardians of the Poor, and many of them had also represented the Council on other bodies.

By 1947 it was obvious that the problems of peace were not going to be solved quickly and it was time for younger members to take over. By that time three senior Aldermen had already retired. Alderman Wheatley had left the Council on becoming a Member of Parliament; Alderman Bacon had given up his Chairmanship of the Estates Committee, and Alderman W Wheeler, who had retired from the headmastership of Broadstone School over 20 years earlier, was ill and had resigned. In 1947, Alderman Shortt, then 83 years old, also resigned, and no less than three other senior members of the Council died that year. Alderman G W Green, the confectioner, of 65 High Street, Alderman Adolphus Shutler, the clothier, of 19 High Street, and Alderman H W Crabb and councillor H D Hunt died shortly afterwards.

In addition to replacements for these eight members (and despite Lord Kershaw's confident statement at a pre-election Labour Party bazaar that 'There would never be anything but a Labour Government in Britain'), five of the Labour members lost their seats in the local elections that year and were replaced by four new Conservative and one Liberal Councillors.

It was, therefore, a very different Council which came to consider the Development Plan for the three boroughs of Poole, Bournemouth and Christchurch which had then been completed by Professor Sir Patrick Abercrombie. The Professor boldly proposed that the centres of both Bournemouth and Poole should be reconstructed. For Bournemouth, he planned that this reconstruction should be accompanied by the building of a new pier. His proposal for the reconstruction of the centre of the Old Town of Poole included provision for a new road to be built through the properties to the west of High Street. Its purpose was to take traffic from the Quay, over the railway, to a point near the George Hotel in Longfleet. His plan also made provision for the doubling of industry in the town, and for its population to be increased to 130,000 in the twenty years of the plan.

Professor Abercrombie had added a caveat to his proposed wholesale reconstruction of the Old Town. In the detailed planning of its reconstruction, care should be taken to preserve the old buildings of historic or architectural interest. He particularly mentioned West End House, the Georgian house facing St James Church, which was then for sale. He suggested that the Corporation should purchase it immediately to ensure its preservation.

The Council reluctantly agreed to reduce the proposed width of the Quay so that the Town Cellars, the Harbour Office and the Customs House would be unaffected and, without hesitation, agreed to purchase West End House, – only for the Ministry to refuse its sanction for the Council to borrow the necessary money!

But the Council could not stomach Professor Abercrombie's proposal that a new road should be built through the properties at the back of High Street. The demolition of a great number of properties was bad enough, but the thought of traffic being diverted from High Street was even worse. Many of them had businesses in High Street and were quite convinced that the prosperity of the town was largely dependent on the prosperity of those businesses, and they were equally convinced that the success of these businesses depended on traffic being allowed to operate freely through the street. Even when, a little later, under pressure of the Roads & Works Committee, the Council agreed to a one-way system for the buses through the street, it would have nothing to do with the Committee's later proposal to extend the one-way system to private cars: it was rejected by 21 votes to 9. The only restriction which the Council agreed in those early years was a prohibition of parking in the narrower, 16-foot wide, length of the street.

But it was not these 'bread-and-butter' topics which excited the Council and the people of Poole in 1947, but the proposal of the Bournemouth Council to ask

Top: West End House today. *Bottom:* The narrow High Street.

the Boundary Commission to incorporate the Borough of Poole into the County Borough of Bournemouth.

The Town Clerk had reported to the Council on the provisions of the Act in December, 1946, but, as the Commission had chosen to review the northern areas of the country first, it was not expected to visit the southern counties until 1948 at the earliest.

Even so, in February, 1947, Bournemouth Council had invited representatives of Poole to discuss the questions which might arise. The members of the two Councils met, but had only discussed matters very generally, feeling that it would be a long time before any definite proposals would have to be made. They had merely agreed that they would endeavour to make proposals which could be supported by each other, and that a further meeting would be held nearer the time of the Commissioners' visit to discuss detailed proposals.

The thought of such a leisurely approach being possible, however, was rudely dispelled in early April by the issue by the Commission of an 'Initiating Notice'. It was served on the Councils of Bournemouth, Poole and Christchurch, the County Councils of Dorset and Hampshire, and the Rural Districts of Ringwood & Fordingbridge and of Wimborne & Cranborne. The Commission informed the Councils that it intended to hold a meeting on 7th July, at which they were all invited to send representatives to be told how the Commission wished to carry out its inquiry. After the initial meeting, the Commission proposed to hear the proposals of the Bournemouth Council on the following day; to visit Poole on 9th July and the other Councils on the following two days.

On 10th May the Poole representatives were invited to attend a second meeting with the Bournemouth Committee when they were informed that the Bournemouth Committee had decided to recommend its Council to apply to absorb Poole into the County Borough of Bournemouth! The Bournemouth Committee invited the Poole representatives to comment on the proposal before it was submitted to its Council. But the Poole representatives seem to have been too shell-shocked to comment. All they seemed to manage to say was that they had no mandate from the Council to make any comment!

When the Poole members recovered from their shock, their first reaction was to enlist support of its traditional enemy, the County Council. At least, the County Council's strong opposition to its loss of Poole, then accounting for a third of its rateable value, could be relied on. Poole's Sub-Committee made haste to consult the County's Boundary Committee.

The meeting was arranged on 19th May, two days after Bournemouth Council had approved its Committee's recommendation. As the Poole representatives had assumed, the County was incensed by the Bournemouth proposal. It was 'monstrous', one of its members had declared, but it then appeared that the County Council had its own territorial demands. It was proposing that its own boundary should be extended eastwards to the 'logical' boundary of the New Forest.

It was no surprise to the Poole members to hear that the County Council was equally opposed to any application by Poole to be made a County Borough. It was implied, however, by the County Council Committee that, if Poole did not apply for County Borough status, the County would be recommended to support an application to extend Poole's boundaries as far west as the Old Harry Rocks and to include the Parish of Corfe Mullen within the borough and, though it would not recommend the County Council to support any application by Poole to include Wimborne Minster and the western strip of Kinson in the borough, it would recommend the County Council not to oppose such an application.

The Poole Committee spent a long time debating what it should recommend to a specially convened meeting of the Council for the 23rd May. By this time the Commission's report on some of the general tenor of its recommendations seemed to favour increased areas of non-county boroughs, rather than the creation of county boroughs. The Committee thought that the Commission was therefore likely to agree to an extension of the area of the town, especially if supported by the County Council, but not, perhaps, its elevation to County Borough status.

Even so, the Committee decided 'after long deliberation' that the Council should consider applying for the grant of county borough status. The Commission's time-table, however, gave them only six weeks to prepare its case. It would need, the Committee thought, at least two or three months for 'the formulation of such representations as the Council consider it necessary to submit after careful and mature consideration of all the relevant factors', and it decided to ask the Commission to defer its hearings until September.

The officers of the Corporation, however, did not delay in providing the Commission with the statistics of the town which had been requested, and they were as follows:

Medical: The present staff included
4 Medical Officers with Consultants part-time
2 Dental Officers & 1 to be appointed
8 Health Visitors (school nurses & child life visitors)
10 Municipal Midwives
6 Sanitary Inspectors
An Infectious Diseases Hospital of 80 beds (taking cases from Blandford, Wareham, Swanage & rural areas).
13 Child Welfare Centres
10 Driver-attendants for the ambulances

1 Rodent Control Officer
3 Operatives

Education: Education was provided for about 10,000 children, and 1 additional Secondary School was being built.
4 Infant School sites were being planned.
2 Grammar Schools (600/700) were being planned.
1 County College & Technical Institute.

Water: Water is provided to 70,000 customers, and bulk supplies to Studland (Corfe Mullen and Lytchett Minster).
The Ministry has requested the Corporation to supply Shapwick and Lytchett Matravers.
In addition, 750,000 gallons a day are provided to the Royal Naval Cordite Factory.

Sewerage: 40% of the area of Poole is sewered which includes 76,000 people. The sewage of Wallisdown, Upper Parkstone, Branksome and Branksome Park is discharged into the sea at Branksome Chine. Oakdale, Longfleet, Stanley Green, the Old Town, Lower Parkstone Canford Cliffs and Sandbanks into the sea at Shore Road, all after Chlorination and disintegration.
Disposal works at Broadstone, and a Disposal works at Hamworthy Cesspools are used by 2500 population living at Merley, Oakley to the north of the borough, and Waterloo and Hamworthy to the south-west.
A main drainage scheme was prepared before the war under which it was agreed that Bournemouth would accept the discharge from Poole for treatment at their Kinson works.
The question was re-opened after the war. The scheme then was to take the discharges of Poole, Bournemouth and Christchurch for preliminary treatment before discharge into the sea near Hengistbury head; the inland disposal works at Kinson, Broadstone and Hamworthy to be dealt with later by the joint body.
Bournemouth, pre-war, adopted the scheme in principle.
Bournemouth has now changed its mind, and Poole is left on its own. The scheme for Hamworthy and Upton has already been prepared. Areas to the north of the town are proposed to be dealt with in conjunction with Wimborne and Bournemouth to go to Kinson.

Refuse Collection & Disposal and Street Cleaning:

Top: Corfe Mullen Waterworks.

Bottom: In 1946 the Corporation converted the ground floor of the Guildhall to provide four men's and four women's slipper baths to replace the baths destroyed by enemy action.

In 1938 a new Refuse Disposal Works was built which separates salvageable materials. The rest is burnt and the clinker used for paths.

Town Planning:

1938 The Draft Planning Scheme was submitted to the Ministry
1944 with Bournemouth & Christchurch agreed to obtain a report by Sir Patrick Abercrombie. He proposed a new road from the Quay to be carried over the railway to eliminate the level crossing; that residential development in Poole should be planned to take a population of 130,000; that land should be planned to double the industrial area of the town, and made detailed proposals for the redevelopment of large areas of the Old Town and many old and obsolete houses and other property.

Parks, etc: The Corporation owns 383 acres of parks & open spaces, as well as 366 acres of turbary land for future public use.

Civic Centre:

The Municipal Buildings were completed in 1932 at a cost of £62,000 which form the nucleus of a civic centre which will ultimately include a Town Hall, Central Library, Central Clinic. (The Police Station adjoining the Municipal Buildings was built in 1940).

Beaches: A promenade has been built from Branksome Dene to Chaddesley Wood and there is another pre-war scheme which is not yet built.

Public Conveniences:

There are eleven public conveniences in Poole and another was agreed to be provided in 1946, but lack of materials has prevented its erection.

Baths: There is a public open-air bath, built in 1929. The town's slipper baths where destroyed by enemy action in 1941. Slipper Baths were provided (4 ladies; 4 men) in the Guildhall in 1946.

Cemeteries: Poole Corporation has four cemeteries at Poole, Branksome, Parkstone and Broadstone.

Highways: Poole has some 157 miles of highway, divided as follows:

Class 1 – 21.5 miles
Class 2 – 10.8 miles
Class 3 – 13.9 miles
Unclassified – 76.0 miles
Private Streets – 35.0 miles

The Council added the following statistics about the town:-

	No	Rateable value
Houses and flats	21,243	£447,968
Business prems	1,283	£64,583
Licenses prems and cinemas	159	£25,873
Public Utilities	14	£73,488
Educational & misc	815	£34,319
Derated properties:		
Industrial	137	£8,862 (35,155)
Freight transport	14	£1,151 (5,747)
Crown properties	21	£3,183
	23,686	£659,527

Rates are 18/10d in the £.
1d rate brings in £2,640
Population: 78,540
Rateable value per head £8.7.11d (£8.40)
Rates per head £7.11s.11d (£7.60)
The Net Debt of the Corporation was £1,101,759, including:
Waterworks £185,640
Housing £445,559
Education £134,535

Housing: Present programme is to deal with 760 condemned houses as soon as approval can be obtained to start.
Waiting list for houses 3094.
The target is to build a total of 4,000 Council houses 228 families are housed in requisitioned properties.

A few days before the special Poole Council meeting, Bournemouth Council had approved its Committee's proposals and they had been leaked to the press. The news of Bournemouth's application to annex Poole was slashed across the front page of the Poole Herald and the cat was truly among the Poole pigeons! Immediately, a meeting was called by the Society of Poole Men, the Poole Chamber of Trade and the Poole Rotary Club demanding that the Council immediately make the strongest protest at this outrageous proposal. A 'Poole United Resistance Committee' was formed of representatives of twelve of Poole's leading societies, including all the local political clubs and such strange bed-fellows as the Communist Party of Poole, the Poole Housewives' league, the Rector of Poole (Rev E C Harris) and Eric Putman, the editor of the local newspaper.

The Committee, with the help of Mr H P Smith, the newly-appointed Deputy Archivist, had soon prepared a Manifesto which detailed 15 reasons for rejecting Bournemouth's proposal. Over 15,000 signatures were collected in the first 10 days, to a petition which was worded 'I am a resident of Poole. I wish Poole to regain full control of its affairs in being made a County Borough, separate from Bournemouth'. 8,000 copies of the 12-page manifesto were quickly sold, and stickers proclaiming 'Stop the Bournemouth Grab', appeared all over the town, and a large banner was strung across High Street, proclaiming the town's total rejection of the 'Grab'.

The Council meeting on 23rd May was unanimous in deciding that the Bournemouth application should be opposed 'with the utmost vigour', and it also decided to apply for an extension of Poole's boundaries. It also appointed a special Boundary Committee with power to act and to discuss its boundary application with the representatives of Wimborne, Upton and Corfe Mullen.

The representatives of the Urban District Council of Wimborne were convinced that the future of small authorities was numbered. They decided that if Poole was to be amalgamated with Bournemouth then they would recommend the Council to agree to join Bournemouth but, if Poole was to remain a separate authority, that Wimborne should join Poole. The Parish of Corfe Mullen was divided, but a majority favoured joining Poole.

But, by this time, the Poole Committee, chastened by the leak of Bournemouth's proposals, played its hand very close to its chest, but the Poole Resistance Committee would probably have been pleased with the case it put to the Commission in opposition to the Bournemouth proposals.

It would be difficult to find two neighbouring boroughs with less community of interest than Poole and Bournemouth, the Committee asserted. Professor Abercrombie, it averred, who was an independent and expert planner, had made this point in his report on the planning of Poole, Bournemouth and Christchurch. He had made the point that Bournemouth's special function was to provide a modern seaside resort, whereas Poole, with its great inheritance, was a port, a seaplane base, a manufacturing and export community, and a County shopping centre.

What was more, the Committee added, Bournemouth Council was apathetic in its desire to annex Poole. Even its own Boundary Committee was split on the subject; a minority report had asserted that the area which would result from such an annexation would be too unwieldy and difficult to administer, and that any common problems would be better solved by Joint Boards. In addition to this, the Poole Council continued, at the special meeting of the Bournemouth Council on 15th May, called to consider its Boundary Committee's proposals, there was such a poor attendance that the meeting was adjourned until the 17th of that month and, even then, only 36 of its 60 members had attended, of whom five had voted against the motion.

The Poole Committee contrasted the Bournemouth Committee's disputed decision with the reaction of the public of Poole and the unanimous reaction of the Poole Council to the proposal.

So far, so good. But the Poole Council was itself divided on what was politic to ask of the Commission. Some favoured the view that it would be best to await the further review by the Commission, promised in ten years time, to press for County Borough status, and that it should be better first to ensure its independent existence, even as a Non-County Borough, than risk fighting on both fronts against the County Council and Bournemouth. Certainly, the overt proposal to apply for county borough status was not included in the resolution of the special meeting of the council and, after the meeting in the Municipal Buildings on 9th July with the Commission, there was no report made of what had transpired there, or of what had been said or what the Commission's view was. It was then a case of waiting for the report of the Commission which was not anticipated until sometime in 1948.

These fundamental questions affecting the long-term future of local government in Poole had overshadowed other immediate local government developments. That year the Town & Country Planning Act had come into force. It transferred the ultimate responsibility for town planning from the borough to the County Council. The County Council immediately asked the borough to continue to be responsible for dealing with planning applications, but reserved to itself the duty of producing a Development Plan for the town, even though the Council had already begun to prepare for such a plan by obtaining Sir Patrick Abercromie's recommendations. However, the County Council decided to appoint its own staff to prepare the official plan and the services of Mr Magnus Austin, Poole's planning consultant (who, earlier, had had much to do with the design of the Municipal Buildings), were discontinued.

Even these fundamental issues for the future of the town could not disguise the serious national problems which arose that year. The Government complied with the conditions of the American loan by making sterling convertible in July. But, with the United States being the only country able to supply the goods then in great demand, every country which had money deposited in Britain promptly converted its pounds into dollars. Britain's reserves were disappearing so quickly that the decision to make sterling convertible had to be quickly reversed.

It was then not only Britain, but the whole of Europe which was in distress. The American Secretary of State, General Marshall, proposed that if the European countries could agree a plan for recovery, he would ask Congress to finance it. By the end of the year the European states had a plan which, they decided, would take $29 billion to implement. General Marshall and President Truman were left with the difficult task of obtaining Congress's approval.

Meanwhile, Britain had to do its best to survive. The Sunday prior to the Boundary Commission's visit to Poole had been declared by the Government as a National Day of Prayer. The Mayor and Corporation attended St James. The Government did what it could to economise. It gave up its Mandate in Palestine and withdrew its forces from Greece. Already it had told local authorities that only works regarded as so important that they ought to be undertaken even in those stringent conditions, should be submitted for approval. No further applications for house building or schools would be approved, it was announced, authorities must concentrate their efforts on the completion of those buildings which had already been commenced. Consumption of fuel had to be restricted, and street lighting must not consume more than 50% of pre-war consumption. Local authorities were to intensify their efforts to collect more salvage. The need for scrap metal and kitchen waste was then as urgent as at any time in the war, and regular collections were essential, the Ministry warned.

As if this was not enough, the winter that year started early and was the harshest since 1880. Farms were cut off by snow, coal supplies ran out and sub-zero weather continued week after week. Factories had to be closed for lack of fuel and power cuts became a regular feature of life as electricity generating stations could not cope with the demand. This led to frequent interruption in the supply of water as water pumps lost their electricity supply, and the Corporation had to warn consumers to keep an emergency supply ready in their houses.

But there was at least one event to brighten the national gloom that year. On 20th November Princess Elizabeth married Philip, Duke of Edinburgh. A collection was made among the members of the Council and the senior officers of the Corporation to buy a wedding present and, on 7th November, the Corporation sent it with a loyal address to the Princess, in which it hoped '*your Royal Highness will on this happy occasion be graciously pleased to accept our gift of a dinner service and vase in Poole Pottery as a token of our loyalty, affection and high esteem.*'

Top: HM Queen Elizabeth II.

Bottom: HRH The Duke of Edinburgh.

Top: A Poole based Sunderland flying boat. *Bottom:* The crew coming ashore.

1948

LET THE BELLS PEAL!

'Poole will be able to continue her steady growth to greater and greater prosperity.'

(*Poole Herald, March, 1948*)

In March, 1948, the Boundary Commission issued its second report. Poole, with nine other towns, was recommended for promotion to County Borough status. The Commission had decided that it was important first to settle the status of councils before tackling the contentious problems of boundary changes.

The Council and, to judge by the Poole Herald's reaction, the general public of Poole, were delighted with the Commission's recommendation to Parliament. It was the Council's greatest ambition to rectify the blunder of its predecessor in 1880 in not opting to claim this status, and it seemed only appropriate that the town should receive this news in the year of the 7th centenary of the grant of the town's first charter, the 'Longspee' Charter. The Poole Herald splashed the story over its front page 'LET THE BELLS PEAL!' it wrote. *'Rejoice! Poole will be able to continue her steady growth to greater and greater prosperity and happiness of its hard-working population of 80,000. The report of the Boundary Commission lays it down that Poole shall be a County Borough in future on its own yet still in Dorset.'*

The Council minutes had recorded no definite resolution to apply for County Borough status. It was not known whether the Committee had been given a secret mandate to ask for County Borough status, or whether the Committee had used its own initiative to ask for it, for it had been given full power to act. On the other hand, the Commission might have taken it upon itself to recommend the town for its new status. But, however it had been achieved no one then cared; the point was that it at last looked likely that Poole Council would soon achieve its greatest ambition and retrieve its control over local services, many of which had only recently been transferred to the County Council.

It was a very encouraging start to the year, but further developments that year were not so pleasing. After months of rumours that BOAC were considering closing the Poole seaplane base, it finally happened. It was announced that the base was formally to be closed on 31st March, and the operations transferred to Southampton.

The Council had done what it could to retain the BOAC base in Poole for the jobs of 600 men and women had depended on it, but its loss to Poole was not universally deplored. Yachtsmen were anxious for the return of their facilities, and residents living near the harbour were relieved to think that there would be no low-flying aircraft or night-time flying practice and that the great sound of revving engines, which had regularly flooded over the harbour at dawn as aircraft engines were warmed up for take-off, would cease.

However, all the townspeople were sorry to lose the prestige of accommodating such an important service and one which had been so crucial during the dark days of the war. Most of the nations' leaders had flown in and out of the airport during the war. General de Gaulle's frequent arrival at the airport had become a signal to Poole people that there would be an air raid on that or the following day. In June, 1943, Sir Hastings Ismay, the Military Secretary, arrived on the day that the plane in which the actor, Leslie Howard, was shot down on a flight from Lisbon in mistake for Winston Churchill's plane. In August that year the 'Bangor' seaplane landed with Sir Anthony Eden; General Sir Alan Brooke, Chief of the Imperial Staff; Admiral Sir Dudley Pound; Air Chief Marshal Sir Charles Portal and Lord Louis Mountbatten, on their return from the Quebec Conference. In June, 1945, the first prisoners released from the Japanese prison camps had arrived at the port and were followed by many others and by servicemen invalided home from the Far East.

With the closure of the airport the buildings which had been taken over by the BOAC and the Ministry of Civil Aviation were derequisitioned. Carter's Pottery on the Quay had been used as a BOAC reception and departure office and by Poole's Medical Officer of Health for checking the health of incoming passengers and for vaccinating those arriving from countries where smallpox was prevalent and inoculating those coming from countries with cholera.

The Ministry of Civil Aviation had taken over the Poole Harbour Yacht Club at Lilliput and the BOAC had requisitioned the old Poole Library at 4 High Street. There had, too, been a section of Admiralty Intelligence at Carter's Pottery to check arrivals which had, in 1943, intercepted two German spies trying to enter the country. In July that year a man known as Neukermanns, said to be a Belgian national, was arrested by that Section, and 'Oswald Job' was apprehended four months later, and both men were subsequently executed.

In the 8 and a half years during which Poole had been the marine airport of the BOAC, 2194 flying boats had landed in Poole Harbour, bringing in 47,772 passengers, and a similar number had flown out of Poole. The details of these landings was as follows:

Top: The Poole Harbour Yacht Club was derequisitioned in 1948 by the Ministry of Civil Aviation.

Bottom: Cornelia Hospital.

The Baiter Hospital. A drawing by J Atkins,
the grandson of the last matron.

Year	*Aircraft landing*	*Passengers*
1939	*15*	*346*
1940	*177*	*2,036*
1941	*125*	*714*
1942	*129*	*3,899*
1943	*229*	*6,306*
1944	*170*	*3,316**
1945	*463*	*11,641*
1946	*373*	*8,617*
1947	*401*	*9,507*
1948	*112*	*2,090*

**In May 1944 BOAC's operations were transferred to Pembroke Dock to leave the Harbour free for the assembly of the Invasion fleet.*

The loss of the airport and its 600 jobs was not the last blow suffered by Poole in 1948. In July that year the National Health Services Act, 1946, came into force. This meant that the Corporation's personal health services, as well as responsibility for health visiting, home nursing and the care of mothers and young children, were transferred to the County Council. That was not all. The Corporation's Infectious Diseases Hospital at Alderney (80 beds) as well as the privately supported Cornelia Hospital (152 beds) and the Parkstone Sanatorium (31 beds) were transferred to the newly appointed Bournemouth & East Dorset Group of the South Western Regional Hospital Board.

The Corporation's smallpox hospital on Baiter peninsula was not wanted by the new board. It decided that any such cases which might arise in the future could well be dealt with at Blandford Hospital. The Council therefore decided to transfer the land at what the Press then called 'the forgotten peninsula' (but was actually an island at high tides!) to the Parks Committee for future use as a public open space. The Parks Committee had no qualms at ordering the demolition of the hospital and the remains of the nissen huts used there by the Forces during the war when Baiter was a 'strong point', guarded by the Home Guard forces of the Poole 'Citadel'.

H P Smith, the Borough Archivist, urged the Council to repair the old Powder House which stood near to the hospital. In 1775 it had been built with the stone from the wall which had previously enclosed the Great Quay to keep the merchantmen's ships' gunpowder at a safe distance from the Quay. But Mr Smith's plea that it should be repaired and maintained as a town monument was ignored by the Committee which was intent on the land being cleared for future use as an open space.

The County Council, however, decided that the personal health services which had then been transferred to it, should be undertaken by a Poole Area Health Sub-Committee, composed of eight county councillors and ten Borough Councillors, with the help and advice of the town's Medical Officer and his staff who had previously been responsible to the borough's Health committee.

These arrangements did nothing to assuage the disappointment of the town's Health Committee and of its staff. The Department had a proud record. It had been its method of immunisation against diptheria, practised in Poole since 1935, which, after being reported to the International Congress of Microbiology the following year, had been adopted by the Ministry of Health in 1940 as the standard recommended practice. The Poole Health Department, too, had had great success in tracking down the source of the local typhoid epidemic of 1936 in which so many local people died, and which had later given the Department much notoriety in the story being dramatised on the BBC.

What was felt most severely, however, was that the town, in losing its Medical Officer of Health had lost its own environmental conscience, a post which the Government had initiated exactly one hundred years ago that year by the Public Health Act of 1848. It was felt as a blow to the town's standing, and made the likely attainment of County Borough status even more important.

The Health Committee of the council and its Medical Officer were disappointed with the provisions of the Health Services Act. They considered that the provisions of the Act, concentrating on the cure of illness, rather than the prevention of disease, had obscured the achievement of the local authorities' public health services which, they considered, had saved more lives in the previous hundred years than the rest of the health services. If more of the vast monies involved in the new service had been directed to the prevention of disease, the Medical Officer later wrote in his formal report, there would soon have been a marked improvement in the nation's health. Preventive medicine had been made the Cinderella of medicine, he fulminated. It meant that, in future, fewer doctors would take the Diploma of Public Health because service in preventive medicine would become less financially attractive. The Act, he added, would be more correctly called 'The National Sickness Act'!

But at least the environmental health duties were left with the Borough. The Health Committee changed its name to the 'Public Health Committee' and agreed to hire back the services of its Medical Officer and his Deputy for one day a week to be responsible for the environmental services of the Corporation, which included the work of the Sanitary Inspectors who remained officers of the Corporation.

The newly-named public Health Committee could then at least concentrate its efforts on environmental problems. It decided, in view of complaints of dust emanating from the gasworks and the Gas Company's open conveyor (which transported coal from the Quay to its Pitwines works through the properties to the east of High Street), and because of the early completion of the new Electricity Generating Station, that stations to measure the amount of soot, ash and grit in the air, should be established in the Old Town, Longfleet and Poole. Though it had powers to prosecute persons who allowed the air to become polluted, it had been given no powers to prosecute industrial users, the likely offenders. In the case of industrial users, all the Corporation could do was to refer the evidence to the Alkali Inspector for attention!

There was, too, another Act which came into force in 1948 which affected many members of the Council. It was the National Assistance Act, 1948, which came into operation in July that year. It was the Act which ended the Poor Law and, with it, the Guardians' Committee and the use of St Mary's Hospital, the old Longfleet Union Workhouse, which had 104 beds which the Board had used as a geriatric hospital. In future, it was enacted, poverty was to be dealt with by the National Assistance Board and local rates. Accommodation and welfare of the poor of Poole was to be the responsibility of the County Council. The Poole Council was given the remnant of the old Guardians' duties, the duty to ensure that solitary people in need of care and attention were taken into care, and the duty to make suitable arrangements for the burial of the dead when there was no one else to carry out this duty.

But, as the Council awaited anxiously for its elevation to the rank of County Borough and the return of its lost powers, the Poole Industrial Advisory committee and the industrialists of Poole had been making solid progress. Wessex Industries had taken over the premises of the old Dolphin Brewery in West Street to produce fork-lift trucks; Ancon Ltd, making aircraft parts, and Northey Rotary Compressors had been established in Alder Road; Southern Textile Engineering, with premises off Levet's Lane, converted its manual machines to being power-driven; Wallis Tin Stamping had expanded at Sterte and was so busy that it was working night shifts; Decca Records had occupied premises at Holton Heath to make slow-playing records for export, and the Hants & Dorset Mineral Water Co at the corner of West Street and Levet's Lane was in full production.

The well-established firms of Poole were also making good progress. Christopher Hill, the millers, had bought the site of the old Belben Mill which had for so long dominated the Quay, and the company was planning to build new premises there; Hamworthy Engineering had arranged with the Corporation to build a sea wall on the Hamworthy side of the Quay so that its site could be extended; Sharp Jones, the pottery established as far back as 1853 at Branksome, was expanding by erecting a new pipe factory facing Poole Road. In addition, the Board of Trade had converted its Royal Ordnance Factory in Sopers Lane to make ceramic goods for the housing drive, and Humphris

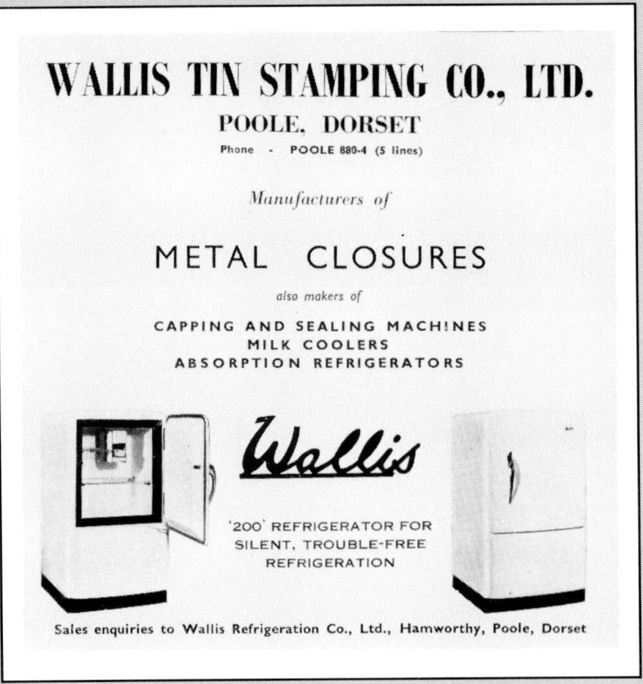

Top: Advertisement for Wallis Tin.

Bottom: Advertisement for Sharp Jones Pottery.

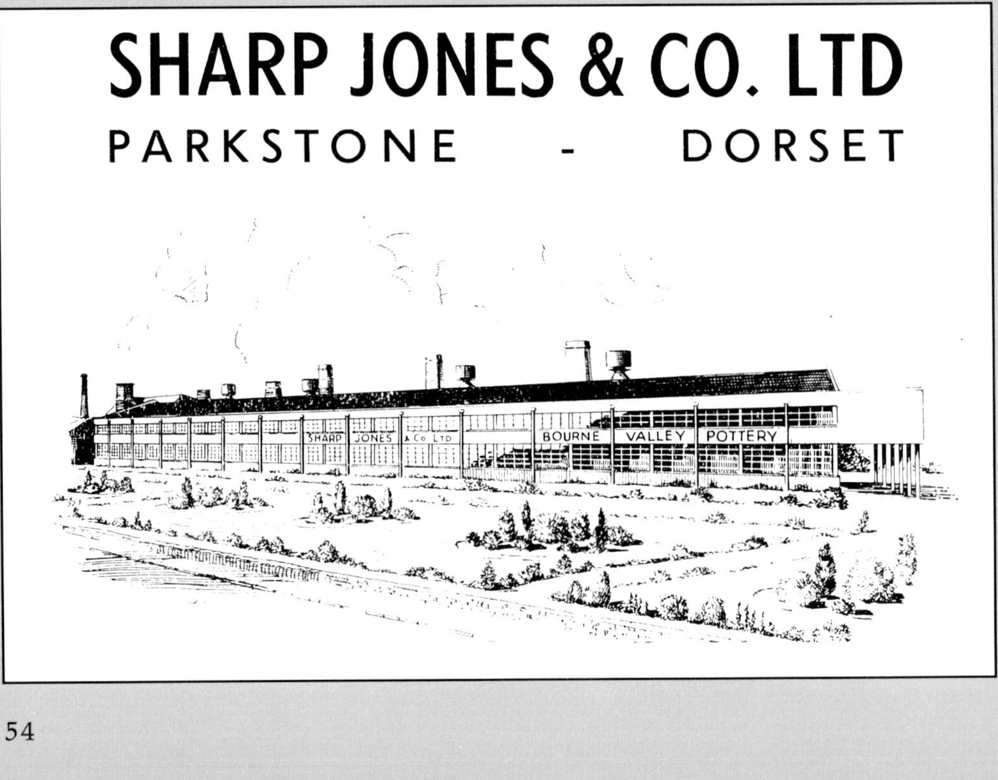

Engineering which made spanners and pressed steel products, famous for its 'Humphris Press', had persuaded the Board of Trade to allow it to build a new large factory off Old Wareham Road, near the factories of the British Diamond Wire Co, Bourne Steel and Chalwyn Lamps.

It was an impressive beginning to Poole's post-war revival, and had been achieved despite the Government's refusal to grant building licences to new firms wishing to come to the area. Only towns with high unemployment were given such licences, and Poole then, despite all its earlier forebodings, could not claim to have high unemployment. This was shown that year by the report of the Education Committee's Juvenile Employment Sub-Committee. In September 1948, at the end of the school year, the Committee reported that of the 393 boys and girls leaving school that year, only 46 of them had not then found employment, and that many vacancies which had been reported to the Committee were still unfilled.

However, the Industrial Advisory Committee had not rested on its laurels. In June that year, it had organised an Industrial Exhibition in Poole Park entitled 'Poole Can Make It'. Fifty-six industrial undertakings of the town erected tents in the Park to demonstrate to the townspeople and the young people of the town the wide variety of goods which were made and the opportunities for employment which were available.

But even this success had its downside. In December of that year the Board of Trade wrote to the Council warning it that, in preparing its Development Plan, little extra land should be shown for industrial development. No large industrial undertakings would be allowed to set up in the town, it warned, and any increased industrial activity would only come from the expansion of existing industries. The Board confirmed that any future grant of building licences would be strictly on the basis of the extent of unemployment in the town, and, as Poole's unemployment was then negligible and, in the Board's opinion, was likely to continue to be negligible, it would be advisable not to zone any further areas of the town for industrial development.

The Council did not agree with the Board of Trade. It was true that unemployment had been comparatively low, but it had been increasing. In 1945 the average monthly unemployment in the town was 71, but it had increased every year since then. In the following three years it had averaged 246, 360 and 498 respectively. What was more, the Royal Ordnance factory employing 600 people, was only a stop-gap use and would probably shortly cease production. In addition the future of Humphris Engineering was then becoming doubtful as its large new factory had been left unoccupied.

But, in any case, the times were not propitious for expansion. Though the financial state of the nation had improved since the United States Congress had approved the grant of Marshall Aid in March that year, the international situation had seriously deteriorated. In February, Russia seized Czechoslovakia by force and, in June, Russian forces closed all rail and road links into Berlin. American B-29 bombers arrived in Britain and the US and Britain flew a shuttle service of supplies over Russian-occupied Germany to feed the people of Berlin, and Europe was again close to war.

In August of that year the Government, fearing war, ordered that no further public air raid shelters or emergency water tanks should be demolished and that no further action should be taken to abandon buildings needed for Civil Defence. It also ordered that the collection of Morrison shelters should be abandoned, that a return should be made to the Ministry of the numbers already collected and these should be returned to Government stores. (This last directive presented the Corporation's officers with a good chance to use their ingenuity as they, in pursuance of the war-time maxim of 'Make do and Mend', had already used the shelter tops to build a perimeter safety wall for the speedway track at the Stadium!)

During all this time, however, the Council's Boundary Committee had steadily prepared its case for the future boundaries of the borough to be presented at a series of meetings which had been arranged by the Commission in July that year. The Committee had been galvanised to further action by the Bournemouth Council which, despite the report of the Commission, decided to press its claim for Poole and Christchurch to be added to its boundaries. The Bournemouth Committee's recommendation to its Council was opposed there by Councillor Sommerbee on the ground that Bournemouth was a health and pleasure resort, whereas Poole was an industrial town and 'two should not marry'. But the majority of Bournemouth Council was determined to have another try and its Committee's recommendation to continue to press its claim to incorporate Poole was carried by 35 votes to 16 at its Council meeting.

By this time Poole had no ally. All sides were refusing to discuss the matter. The Poole Committee even refused an invitation to meet the County Council Committee prior to its interview with the Commission. It was, perhaps, also symptomatic of the feelings between the members of the authorities that Bournemouth Council then refused to renew the reciprocal arrangements which had been made between the two Councils during the war to allow taxis registered in one town to pick up passengers in the other. In future, Poole taxis were no longer allowed to pick up fares in Bournemouth.

The Poole Committee, however, did continue to consult neighbouring authorities affected by its own boundary proposals. As could be anticipated, Poole's own ideas of incorporating other areas were not universally welcomed. The vote by the Parish of Corfe Mullen on the proposition that it should join Poole, for instance, was carried by 41 votes to 18 in July, but those against the proposal pressed the matter to a meeting of the parishioners at Lockyer's School

Top: Another example of Poole's 'Make do & Mend' activities was this breakwater at New Quay, using landing craft left in the harbour.

Bottom: Branksome Tower Hotel was re-opened at Whitsun, 1948. It had been used by the American Army from 1943.

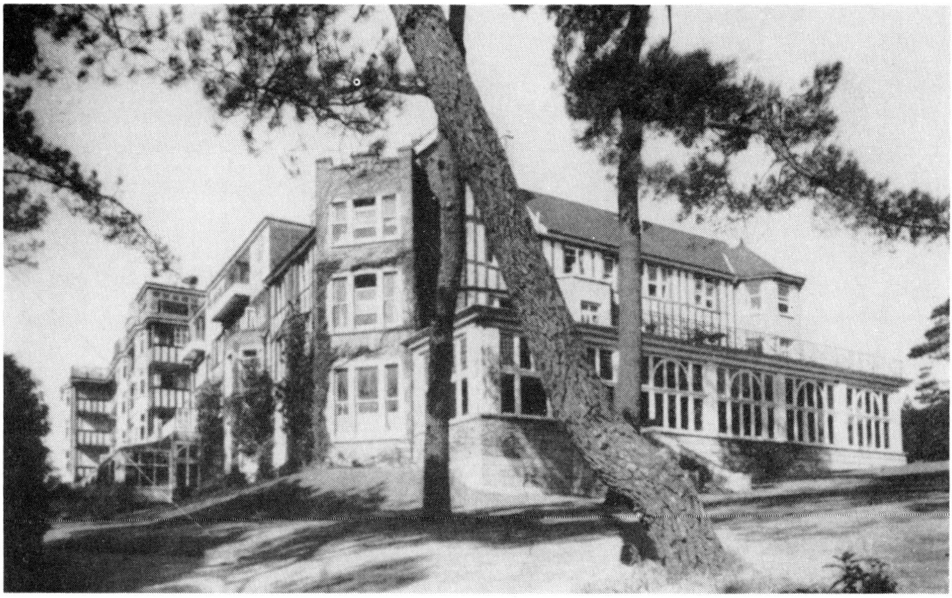

Top: Alderman Herbert Carter, OBE and Freeman of Poole, resigned in 1948 after being an Alderman since 1905. After being Sheriff in 1906/7 he had been Mayor five times.

Bottom: Poole Park Miniature Railway. Despite criticism that the railway would drive the swans and ducks from the Park, the Council, in 1948, licensed the railway, subject to receiving 25% of the takings, with charges of 1/– (5p) for adults and 6d ($2\frac{1}{2}$p) for children.

where it was carried only by the narrow majority of 64–62 and, even then, the opponents were claiming that that meeting had been improperly called.

However, Poole decided to stick to its original proposals for the extension of the Borough. It wanted the western part of Kinson, including the main approach road to the north to be taken from Bournemouth and added to Poole and, to the west, Corfe Mullen and Upton so that the southern boundary of Poole should follow the perimeter of the harbour on the high tide mark which would then include Arne and Studland as well as the islands of the harbour.

After the further meeting with the Commission, it was then again a case of waiting for the result. But, as the year came to an end, yet another Act affecting local government came into effect. The Representation of the People Act decreed that in future local elections would no longer be held in November, but in May. The service of existing members of the Council and its Mayor and Sheriff were extended to May, 1949, and, by the Act, Councillor Bravery became the first Poole Sheriff ever to serve more than a year in the office.

By and large, the year had been a very good one for Poole. It was in sight, at last, of attaining its great ambition to be a County Borough, which would mean the return of the powers and duties which it had lost in the previous few years. In addition to this, Parliament that year agreed to its Constituency Boundary Commission recommendation, among which was that Poole should become a single, 'Poole', constituency. Again, its Town Clerk was to be responsible for preparing the Electoral Register for the town; its Sheriff was again to become Returning Officer for Parliamentary elections, and Poole was again to have its own Member of Parliament.

Top: Council houses built by John Laing & Co in Wallisdown Road.

Bottom: Sylvan Road School.

1949

WHA'S M'AR WI' POOLE?

'I stood by the gates at mid-day on my
way down the High Street of Poole.
I have noticed, when wishing to hurry, the
gates are fast-closed as a rule,
And I thought how this irksome obstruction
must keep the town back in its trade,
How the hours upon hours that are wasted
must eat up the profits it made,
It's a curse on the place and a scandal that
the traffic must ever delay
And yet the town takes it calmly, – is there
nothing to do or to say?'

(Herbert Carter, 'Wha's M'ar Wi' Poole', 1926)

In 1949 life in Britain became no easier. Marshall Aid had avoided disaster, but the nation's underlying problems remained. Sir Stafford Cripps' 'Austerity Budget' set income tax at 9/- (45p) in the £, and he had imposed a 'once-and-for-all' levy on the 'rich'. He said, though, that taxation had then reached 40% of the nation's total income, and could go no higher without taxing the very people who were the recipients of the social services. 'We must, therefore' he said, 'moderate the speed of our advance in the extended application of existing services to our progressive ability to pay for them by an increase in our national income'. He had, however, an almost impossible task in trying to balance the nation's accounts, for the National Health Service alone, in its first year of operation, had overspent its budget by £52m.

In May there was some relief when the Russians lifted their blockade of Berlin, but pressure on the pound continued unabated and, in September, the pressure on it became so intense that Sir Stafford Cripps felt driven to devaluation. He devalued the pound from $4.03 to $2.80 to the £, and, inevitably, the cost of most things rose. The gold sovereign became worth 58/- (£2.90); the price of a loaf of bread rose to 5½d from 4½d, the price of school meals was increased to 6d (2½p) from 5d (2p); the price of the local 'Echo' rose to 'three half-pence', and interest payable on loans to the Corporation from the Public Works Loan Board rose from 2% to 2½% and, most controversially, a charge of 1/- (5p) was levied on National Health prescriptions.

These national developments inevitably affected the work of the Council, for the financial problems of the nation brought any further acquisitions or approvals to an abrupt stop. The earlier 'Stop' of 1947 had been reversed to 'Go' in 1948 and the Council had obtained the promise of approval to build a further 500 council houses. The Committee, then fretting at the continuing delays in the completion of houses, for which lack of supplies were blamed, had entered into a contract with John Laing & Co to build non-traditional houses at Wallisdown. It therefore happened that, on the Government's 'Stop' notice in 1949, the Corporation's immediate programme was not greatly affected. It was, therefore, able to end 1949 having built 1256 houses (including the 200 'pre-fabs' which had then been installed), and had many in contract. In addition 440 houses had been built privately and a further 244 units of accommodation had been provided by the conversion of houses into flats.

Housing, though, was not the only casualty of the Government's financial restraints. The same blanket refusal of any further school building was announced. What was more, the Ministry added, economies were to be made in the running costs of education. So far as building contracts was concerned, the Council was again relatively unscathed for the immediate future. Herbert Carter Secondary School was then so far advanced that 300 pupils had already been able to be accepted into the school, and the building of Sylvan Road School and Trinidad Primary were in contract. Nor was the Committee forced into reductions of the Evening Classes then held at four schools and at which 815 pupils attended. But the Education Committee had to find other economies, and it was decided to close two of its three Nursery Classes and to economise in the expense of providing transport of scholars. If children over 8 years old lived within three miles of their school they were no longer offered free school transport, and even children under 8 had to live more than 2 miles from school to obtain free bus passes.

Similar economies had to be made in the other Committees of the Council. The Parks Committee, for instance, in its anxiety to bring its parks and open spaces back to their peacetime condition, wished to re-erect the cast-iron railings round Poole and Parkstone Parks which had earlier been surrendered for the war effort, but the Ministry would not consider such an unessential expense. The Committee, too, was anxious to get rid of the 60 ft oil tank erected in the relative safety of the park in the war to hold fuel for the motor torpedo boats stationed at the Quay, but felt it could not press for its removal while the Gas Company insisted it was essential for their gas supplies. The Committee was also frustrated in its attempt to get back possession of the Ladies Walking Field at Seldown from the allotment holders, having been persuaded by the Ministry that it was essential to retain as many allotments as possible for the sake of food production.

Certainly, food was then at a premium. The Parks Committee had the greatest difficulty in obtaining a reasonable quantity of supplies to keep its beach cafes operational. On the Ministry of Food refusing its request to increase its ration of foods, Alderman Bright, the Chairman of the Committee, supplied cakes from his bakery in High Street to the cafes, only to have the mortification of being accused in Council of profiteering at the Council's expense! But, perhaps, the best illustration of the difficulties of those days was the formal acceptance by the Council of a Parks Committee resolution to apply to the Food Control Committee for an allocation of food so that the swans in Poole Park could be fed!

These difficulties probably had much to do with the Parks Committee's decision that the cafes would be better operated by the lessee. It issued an advertisement asking for offers to take on rent its cafes at Sandbanks, Branksome Chine, Branksome Dene Chine and Cliff Cafe Lodge for a term of $4\frac{1}{2}$ years. It received no offers at all in response to this advertisement, so the invitation was re-advertised, this time for a lease of seven years. On this occasion an offer of £3,000 a year was received from Antonio Forte, a local man who operated beach cafes in other southern towns, but his offer was subject to the Corporation giving him an option, at the expiry of the seven year term, to extend it for a further seven years. The Committee agreed and recommended the Council to accept these terms.

There had already been some opposition by the Labour members to the principle of letting the management of the cafes go out of Council control. It came to a head when the Parks Committee recommendation came before the Council for ratification. 'This report tells every member of the Council precisely nothing!' cried Alderman Reeves, the Labour leader on the Council. 'We are here solemnly meeting to say 'Yes' to something we know nothing about. They are handing over the cafes in the same way as they handed over the 'buses!'

But, although Alderman Reeves lost his motion for the Council to reject the Committee's recommendation, it was not the end of the matter. A few days later, at the behest of two members of the public, a local firm of solicitors issued a High Court writ, alleging that the Corporation was acting illegally in, effectively, letting its cafes for 14 years without having first obtained the approval of the Ministry. It was a true bill. The Corporation did need Ministry approval for leases over 7 years. The Committee, though, was able to negotiate itself out of the dilemma by obtaining Mr Forte's agreement to leave the lease at a straight seven years and, eventually, the lease was executed.

Top: Councillor Arthur Lloyd-Allen.

Bottom: Alderman D A Haynes.

The reference of Alderman Reeves in 'handing over the buses' referred to the Corporation's earlier ownership of the Poole Tramway. It had bought it when the private company's efforts to extend the lines through Bournemouth had been foiled in 1905. Having bought the undertaking, the Corporation had then joined with the Bournemouth Corporation in forming a joint operation. However, thirty years later, when Bournemouth Council, as operator, decided to do away with the trams and substitute a trolley-bus service, Poole Council had jibbed. It had feared the effect on the town of festooning its roads with the wires necessary for the trolley buses, and drew out of the joint agreement.

However, having retrieved its tramway and its right to run public transport through the main roads of the town, the Corporation had then let its rights to the Hants & Dorset Omnibus Co to operate the service with its petrol-driven buses. It was an agreement which in the late 1940's was providing the Corporation with an income of around 1,750 a year, but it was a lease which the Labour faction on the Council felt should never have been granted. The lease, however, had given the Council's Transport Committee the right to become involved with the Bus company in the setting of fare stages and the siting of bus stops and shelters and, with its Transport Officer, became intimately involved in the details of the services and fares charged in Poole.

The reference by Alderman Reeves in his early outburst about the proposed lease to Forte's that the minute told the Council 'exactly nothing' probably referred to the slack working which had crept into the minuting of Committee decisions. Councillor Lloyd-Allen, an accountant who had returned from war service to practise in Parkstone and who had been elected for the Parkstone Ward in November, 1948, to fill the vacancy occasioned by Councillor D A Haynes' election as Alderman, had been making the point for some time that Committee minutes often did not make clear what had been decided. At various Council meetings he had quoted many examples and included such phrases as 'The Town Clerk reply in the manner mentioned'; 'The matter be left in the hands of the Town Clerk'; and 'The minutes of the meeting be amended as now detailed'. He pleaded for accuracy and intelligibility, and the abolition of what he called 'minutese'.

It was a point which the Poole Herald enjoyed enlarging upon. But, the paper always enjoyed a dig at members of the Council and, after agreeing with Councillor Lloyd-Allen's criticisms, it added 'at the same time, there will be a lot of sympathy for the unfortunate minute clerks, whose job is to make sense out of the deliberation of Councillors, some of whom would have a job to pass a 14 year old's exam in English'!

In the Government's great concern to make all economies possible, its Ministries had obviously been asked to keep a close eye on all local government action which might waste money or resources. One of the more bizarre examples of this was a letter from the Ministry of Fuel & Power to the Town Clerk of Poole. It had been noticed, it said, that the Poole Corporation had licensed 50% more taxis in 1949 than it had prior to the war, and it wanted an assurance from the Town Clerk that all these taxis were being used as such, and that private owners had not applied for taxi licences, merely to get the extra petrol ration given on taxis!

But, petrol rationing and the lack of new cars (then on a two to three years' delivery time) notwithstanding, cars were already causing problems in Poole. The most serious one was the congestion caused by the railway level crossing gates over High Street and Towngate Street. The inevitable delays played havoc with the Bus timetables as the buses tried to return to their station at 'White's Place' (Beech Hurst), near the Public Library. The Committee took a census over 6 working days of the closing of the gates which showed the following closures of the gates:

TOWNGATE LEVEL CROSSING:

	Motor vehicles	Horsedrawn	Cycles	Total	Times closed
8am–6pm	*17,568*	*325*	*5,119*	*27,0123*	*359*
Average					
per day	*2,928*	*54*	*1,520*	*4,502*	*60*
per hr	*293*	*5*	*152*	*450*	*6*

HIGH STREET LEVEL CROSSING:

	Motor vehicles	Horsedrawn	Cycles	Total	Times closed
8am–6pm	*21,580*	*367*	*27,189*	*49,136*	*312*
per day	*3,597*	*61*	*4,531*	*8,189*	*52*
per hour	*360*	*6*	*453*	*819*	*5*

The average time that the gates were closed was just over 3 minutes.

The Committee and the Bus Company agreed that it was essential to move the bus station to the other side of the railway and that this could be accommodated in a widened Kingland Crescent where ten bus lay-bys could be established and a bus station could be built when a licence could be obtained. The Bus Company agreed to pay 70% of the costs involved.

The level crossings, however, were not the only traffic hazard created by the railway in the Old Town. Its railway line which led from Poole station through Nile Row, down West Quay Road and then crossing the road near Poole Bridge to the Quay constituted a grave impediment to the free passage of cars, and the

Top: The two level crossings. *Bottom:* The quay railway.

trucks which were often left on the line, unlit at night, were a constant danger. The Committee made many complaints, even enlisted the help of learned counsel, to get the railway at least to light the trucks at night, but it was all to no avail.

Other Committees of the Council, however, had more success. The Planning Committee, for instance, became concerned as to how to deal with applications which were then being received for the development of parts of Branksome Park. An earlier permission had been negated by the Branksome Park Association winning a High Court action to enforce the restrictive covenant that only houses in an acre of land should be built in the Park.

The Committee initiated negotiations with the Branksome Park Association to break the deadlock, for it seemed absurd that planning applications which the Committee considered appropriate should be negated by the Association.

The negotiations were concluded in 1949. It was agreed that for planning purposes the park should be divided into six areas. In two of these areas the covenant that only dwellinghouses would be permitted was retained, except that the curtilage could be reduced to three-quarter of an acre. In another area new blocks of flats or guest houses would be permitted; one area was to be reserved for new blocks of flats, one for new hotels, and the remaining area reserved for private or public open spaces. Any new blocks of flats were to contain a maximum of 16 flats to the acre, and the block was not to cover more than one-sixth of the site; the building was to be at least 50′ from the road and at least 30′ from its nearest neighbour.

The Committee, however, was aware that a more intensive development of the Park could constitute a danger to the wooded character of the area. It therefore decided to obtain expert advice on the subject, and appointed James Best, the Honorary Tree Consultant of the Dorset County Council, for a report on the trees of the area.

James Best reported that 'the 700 acres of Branksome Park was peculiar and almost unique in that its trees formed a wood inside a residential area, and was only comparable to the Tiergarten in the middle of Berlin'. The trees, he reported, were mainly Scottish pines, with a few broad leafed species, such as chestnut, oak and robinia, with rhododendrons forming a fairly dense undergrowth. Most of these trees were near their maximum growth but not over-mature, but could, in places, be discreetly thinned. However, he added, indiscriminate felling could have serious consequences from the effect of gales.

The Committee decided that Preservation Orders should be made to cover the whole area of the Park so that any applications to fell trees could then be considered on their merits after a report from the Parks Superintendent. It was a decision which was followed up over the following years to be applied to cover all the wooded ares of the town.

In other areas of the Council's responsibilities, the Council also had some success. One was obtaining loan sanction to make-up some of the gravelled builders' roads of the borough to such a standard that they could be taken over as roads repairable at the public expense. This meant levelling and consolidating the roads after putting in a system of surface water drainage to take away rainwater, tarmacing them and putting in footpaths and street lighting.

Very many miles of these gravelled "builders" roads had been laid down prior to the war and were then in a ruinous condition. The local newspaper had a field day each rainy period reporting on the effects of the weather on the roads, usually accompanied by photographs of children tiptoeing between the puddles as they went to school or of cars stuck in the enormous ruts which had developed. Members of the Council duly brought the complaints before Council. The old campaigner, Alderman A J Dacombe, even managed, on some pretext of another, to raise the condition of Good Road at every meeting of the Council.

1949, as it happened, however, was a year of severe drought. It was worse than the 'drought years' of 1921 and 1924, but it brought no respite to the weight of complaint of the condition of the roads, for the continuing dry conditions meant that clouds of dust rose behind every passing vehicle brave enough to traverse the roads!

The very seriousness of the condition of the roads at least allowed the Council, armed with the Medical Officer of Health's certificate that their condition constituted a danger to health, to persuade the Ministry to allow it to borrow enough money to attend to some of the worst roads. After all, the Corporation could argue, the loan would be soon repaid as the costs were to be apportioned between the owners of the properties which fronted the roads.

That sounded a good argument for obtaining the Ministry's approval but, in practice, it was not quite so easy. Tenants were only too anxious to have their roads made up, but owners, who had to pay their share of the costs, were often not so anxious when they obtained their provisional apportionments of cost. What was more, the Council had adopted a system of varying the apportionments made on the actual frontage of the property concerned by the degree of benefit which it was thought to obtain from the work having been done, and this led to many objections being made to the provisional apportionments.

The result was that few roads on which provisional apportionments had been made were not contested in the Magistrates' Court. Even the Magistrates' decision was not always agreed. A few objectors pursued their case to Quarter Sessions and, in those early years, three objectors even pursued their case to the High Court, – after which the Poole Corporation had the dubious distinction of providing the majority of Case Law on the subject of Private Street Works!

The drought, however, had caused other problems. Poole Corporation's Water Undertaking, unlike many others in the country did not have to restrict

Top: Richard Rendle, Poole Waterworks Engineer.

Bottom: Branksome Park, The Avenue.

supplies but already, in view of the ever increasing demands for water, the Water Department had, under the energetic lead of its Water Engineer, Richard Rendle, been exploring the hinterland of Poole to find an additional supply. It had chosen a point in Sturminster Marshall where a large underground lake would ensure a plentiful supply of water for the foreseeable future. The Committee agreed detailed plans for the new well and pumping station and had submitted them with an estimated cost (£130,000) to the Ministry.

Instead of giving permission to borrow the money to build its new works, the Ministry asked the Council to approach surrounding district Councils with a view to Poole supplying their residents with a piped-water supply.

The Council was not anxious to do so, for it was a costly business to supply rural areas. Long lengths of pipe were required to serve the dispersed properties and the Corporation's charge of 2/6d (12½p) in the £ on the rateable value of the properties served could hardly be a self-balancing operation, in view of the low rated rural properties. That would mean that the balance would have to be paid by the rest of the consumers in Poole, a situation which was already happening, in the view of the Poole Council, in the case of other services which had been recently taken over by the County Council.

However, the Council agreed to initiate negotiations with the nearby District Councils and these were successful in the case of Shapwick, Sturminster Marshall and Lytchett Matravers, but other Councils were suspicious of the Council's motives, – especially, in one case, when a Poole member was quite unable to guess how much water the average cow drank each day!

Other Committees of the Council, however, were not having even partial success. The Government, forever tinkering with its system of paying grants to local authorities, had earlier made part of its grant dependent on the average rateable value per resident. This had led some local authorities' Valuation Committees to temper the wind to its ratepayers by setting the rateable values of properties as low as reasonably possible, in the anticipation that whatever the individual ratepayer saved would be made up by Government grant! It was, therefore, inevitable that there should be some uniform basis of assessing rateable values from Councils and gave the duty to the Inland Revenue. It meant that the Poole Valuation Committee had its last meeting that year and its two valuers transferred their allegiance from the Council to the Inland Revenue.

But transcending all these events in 1949, was the saddening end of the Boundary Commission and all its recommendations. Earlier that year, the Council had got wind of the Government's intentions to scrap the Boundary Commission. It had called on the help of its Member of Parliament, Col Mervyn Wheatley, to arrange an interview with the Minister in which the other nine towns which had been recommended for County Borough status took part. It had, though, been of no avail. It was said that to put the Commission's recommendations into effect would need a new Act of Parliament and, it seemed, the Government had decided that it had enough problems to go on with. Its nationalisation programme had run into difficulties. Lord Lyle, the Poole resident and Chairman of the large sugar firm of Tate and Lyle was putting up a robust fight as 'Mr Cube' against the firm's nationalisation; the Lords had thrown out the Steel Nationalisation Bill and it was certain that the Members of Parliament representing rural areas would oppose an Act establishing new County Boroughs. The Government was quite unprepared to press on with its local government reorganisation. Instead it brought in the Local Government (Boundary Commission Dissolution) Bill, and Poole's great hopes had come to naught, at least temporarily.

There was, too, weighing on the Government, the war in Korea and the real threat of a new war breaking out in Europe. Up till then, despite the Russian's bellicose words and actions, there had been some comfort in the knowledge of the American possession of the atomic bomb. However, that year, the Russians successfully exploded their own atomic bomb, and the West felt even more insecure.

The Government asked local authorities to re-establish their Civil Defence organisations, to cease the demolition of air raid shelters, and to enlist and train volunteers. The Director of Civil Defence Training came to Poole to address members of the Council and others on the necessity of again forming a civil defence corps but, to the Council's indignation, the Government was again following its practice of making the County Council the ultimate 'scheme making authority' for the whole county. In the end, the Poole members and officers were given by the County Council the primary responsibility for the whole of East Dorset, but it was little comfort for the Council which, during the latter stages of the war, had been its own civil defence authority, beholden only to the Government. However, the Council took up its renewed duties, appointed the enthusiastic Jim O'Hara from the St John's Ambulance Brigade as its training officer. But volunteers were found to be much less enthusiastic to join the Corps as they had been in wartime. It was difficult to motivate recruits to undertake the sometimes hazardous training, and Poole never did reach its targets.

By this time, the Government was coming towards the end of its term of office, and seemed to be clearing its slate for an early election. The rationing of clothing was ended in November that year, just as a long-looked for supply of nylon stockings first appeared in the shops; the petrol ration was doubled which allowed car owners petrol to drive 180 miles a month but, ironically, the ration of sweets was reimposed because, it was said, of the 'lack of dollars' – just at the time when sweet rationing was ended in Germany!

But it was not all gloom. The Government, whistling in the wind, announced that a 'Festival of Britain' would be held in 1951 to celebrate the centenary of the

Beating the bounds of Poole Harbour.

Great Exhibition of 1851. But the Poole Corporation had already gone one better. In July, with the Yacht Clubs, it had re-established the Poole Yacht Week which had ended with a firework display at Baiter Point. In August it had held its unique water pageant of the 'Beating of the Bounds of Poole Harbour' when the Mayor, Alderman A B Haynes, the Broadstone pharmacist and Broadstone's first Mayor had, as Admiral of the Port, peregrinated the harbour boundaries in the 'Anzio' and 58 accompanying vessels with his jury to report any infringements to the harbour. Yachts, pleasure boats and anything which could float spent the day sailing round the harbour, accosted by the 'pirates', in a day when the concerns of office and shortages were forgotten.

It was the first time that many of the guests has seen the harbour free from the enormous tyres which marked out the long landing strips of the flying boats. It was, too, the first time that many of the people taking part in the ceremony had seen the 110 yard long pier built by the Admiralty at Round Island which it had used as its Headquarters in the war. The island was then for sale at an asking price of £28,000. It had been given to Major and Mrs Laurence's father, Lord Iliffe, who owned Furzey Island. Edward Maufe, the architect of Guildford Cathedral, had designed a house on the island to which electricity and telephones had been connected, but the major and his wife had emigrated to America to gain 'freedom from the obstructive controls' of Britain.

These ceremonies were not the only ones which the Council planned that year. Miss Llewellin, then Sheriff, who was very involved in the Girl Guide movement in Dorset, proposed, and Alderman Reeves, whose father had been very active in the Boy Scout movement in Upper Parkstone, seconded, that Lady Baden Powell should be offered the Freedom of the Borough: *'in recognition of her service to youth over a period of years in the leadership of the Girl Guide movement, work which had brought health and happiness to the girlhood and young womanhood of all nations throughout the world; And in happy and proud remembrance of her close association with this Borough which enjoys the privilege of being the birth place of scouting and home town of the Chief Guide of the world.'*

Top: Clifton Road viewpoint. The Council agreed that a notice should be erected to state that Mrs Ada Frances Jennings gave this land to the Corporation and to state that 'the woodland had been dedicated to the use and enjoyment of the inhabitants of the borough as a memorial to her husband, the late Thomas Jennings.'

Bottom: Whitecliff Recreation Ground today.

Blue Boar Lane, one of the quay slums
demolished in the fifties.

1950

THE POOLE GENERATING STATION

'The days of Old Poole as a place
to live are numbered.'

(*Poole Herald, 1948*)

The 'Silver Lining' savings campaign of 1949 had not lived up to the Government's implied promise. The general conditions of life in the country had, if anything, got worse. Rationing of most foods was still in force, and the tax on petrol was raised sharply to bring the price of petrol up from 2/3½d (12p) to 3/- (15p) a gallon. The only concession was that the limit of 5/- (25p) on the cost of any meal served in restaurants, which had been in force since 1942, was annulled in an effort to encourage tourists to come to Britain.

By this time there was a primitive, black-and-white television service, but the great majority of people were still firmly committed to the 'wireless', as they had been during the war. One of the most popular programmes then was 'Any Questions', a programme begun by Frank Gillard, controller of the BBC's Western Service from Bristol. One of these programmes was held before an invited audience in the Conference Room of the Municipal Buildings in January that year and Phillis Arney, wife of Peter Arney, a Committee Clerk and Secretary of the Poole Speedway Supporters' Club and of the 'Friends of Poole Hospital', asked a question on the topic which was bothering everybody at the time. She asked 'Why was Britain the only country with food rationing?' None of the distinguished panel of John Arlott, Vernon Bartlett, Ralph Wightman and Graham Hutton, could give a satisfactory answer.

But, as always, most of the problems of the country were rooted in the dire financial situation of the nation. The Cold War in Europe had made it impossible to cut defence costs and, in 1950, when the Communists of North Korea invaded South Korea, the Cold War was spread to the Far East. The Government increased the length of compulsory national service from eighteen months to two years, and defence spending rose again as Britain assembled a 'Composite Force' to join the Americans and Australians to repel the invaders.

The nation's financial predicament had its inevitable effect on local government. As early as January the Ministry cancelled all its approvals for loans for house building for which tenders had not already been accepted. This caught the Poole Council by surprise for it had issued private building licences on the one private licence for every four completed Council houses on the supposition that it would have been able to build at least a further 100 Council houses that year. The Ministry, however, were quick to notice this. It wrote to the Town Clerk, accusing the Council of over-issuing twenty-one licences. No further licences were to be issued, it warned, until the Council had completed a further 225 Council houses. Even when that number of council houses had been completed, it warned, further private licences were to be granted only at the rate of one private house for every ten Council houses completed by the Corporation.

As a further economy, the Ministry also directed that the specification of Council houses was to be reduced. In future, Council houses were to have frontages of no more than 25 feet, rather than the 30 feet previously accepted. What was more, the height of rooms in future Council houses was to be reduced from 8 feet to 7ft 6ins. The Ministry also reduced by 20% the total amount of work which the Council could licence for the maintenance or repair of war-damaged properties.

These further restrictions raised tensions in the Council for, despite all the efforts of the Estates Committee, the waiting list for Council houses was still as high as 3262, little different from what it was in 1946. The members of the Council were frustrated by the ever-increasing delays in the completion of houses. It then had eight building contracts in hand, all of them seriously delayed, some by as much as a year. The members of the Council not themselves involved with the Estates Committee and its problems, could not understand it. They felt that the Estates Committee must be too complacent in agreeing extensions of contracts. They themselves, criticised by the public, for not re-housing more families, claimed that the Estates Committee should be firmer with its contractors. The normally soft spoken Geoffrey Bravery, was sometimes criticised for not being heard in the Council chamber, but there could be no such complaint at a meeting of the Council early in 1951 for, finally exasperated by the criticism, he shouted, 'If any of you want this job, you are very welcome!', but none of his critics was heard to volunteer!

Housing was far from being the only casualty of the economies that were possible in any of its services, and Poole Council set up special 'Economy Committee' which made a number of recommendations. One of its more disputed recommendations was to defer the Slum Clearance scheme for the Old Town.

This recommendation was accepted by the Council, and came as a bitter disappointment to the Public Health Committee and its Medical Officer of Health. It had been pressing the Council to tackle the problem of the Old Town for some time. Conditions there, in 1950, were quite dreadful. Many of the houses had then become derelict. The larger ones had been occupied by a great variety of homeless people, most of them occupying a single room, and the whole area had become a disgrace to the town. Any family which was able to move out of the area did so, often leaving their old house empty, making conditions in the Old Town worse, as it was either vandalised or taken over by squatters. The condition of the Old Town was even worse that it had been two years earlier when the Poole Herald had decided that there was no hope that the Old Town would ever again become an area in which people would be happy to live. 'The days of Old Poole as a place to live are numbered,' it had reported and, it had added by way of proof, that only 193 of the 463 people on the Electoral Roll of St James Parish (the boundary of which was the same as that of Old Poole) still lived in the Parish.

In 1950 the condition of the Old Town was worrying many people. At the annual meeting of the Lagland Street Youth Club, John Liddle, reported that 'there are pockets of vice in Old Poole comparable with anything in Liverpool'. The Rector of Poole agreed that there was 'a lot of vice in Poole, but it is incomparable with Liverpool'. The Borough Youth Officer added his voice. 'Conditions of living and behaviour in some areas of Old Poole would surprise some of the more respectable people of the town, he said. 'You get the condition of a port in miniature'.

The Public Health Committee had been advised that it was an essential prerequisite to the making of a slum clearance order that a detailed study of the sanitary condition of every house be included in such an order. The Committee had therefore persuaded the Council that an extra Sanitary Inspector should be appointed in 1951 whose sole task was to make the necessary survey, and it was this appointment which was a casualty of the Economy Committee's recommendations and, once again, the long task of slum clearance was postponed.

It was, too, only natural for the Economy Committee also to consider maximising the Corporation's income, and it was out of this review that the Council decided for the first time to charge for some of its services. In future, it was decided, there would be a charge of 6d (2.5p) for each morning and afternoon session at its car parks, and that a charge would be made by the Weights & Measures Department of between 3d and 2/- for adjusting the weights and measures used in the town.

But it was not only local government services which were affected by the economy drive. The state of the national economy had not allowed the National Health Service enough money to provide all the facilities which were then being

Top: Alderman AB Haynes.

Bottom: Mrs Attlee, Alderman Reeves and Evelyn King at the opening of the Labour Party's Sports Ground at Fleets.

demanded by the public and the press. Despite the building of a new theatre block at Poole Hospital, the Press reported in January, that 1342 local people were waiting for a hospital bed, and that it was estimated that there was a 59% shortage of hospital beds in the area.

In February there was an uproar in the press about the proposed closing of the Poole Guardians' St Mary's Hospital at Longfleet on the opening of the St Leonard's Hospital, the war-time hospital built by the American Army which had then been handed over to the Health Authority. Only nine of the 150 inmates of St Mary's, the newspaper reported, were happy to be transferred to the distant St Leonard's hospital. Then, in May, the Poole Herald, was again complaining of the health service. 'You have to wait to be ill', it headed its report, and asserted that patients had to wait 16 weeks to see an orthopaedic consultant, and fourteen weeks to see an ear-nose-and-throat consultant.

But the overwhelming concern of those days was the stark fear of another war. It was then thought that the Russians had the atomic bomb, and the West no longer felt safe from attack. This general feeling of apprehension was enhanced by the Government's edict that local councils were to demolish no more air raid shelters and that they were to re-establish their Civil Defence organisations.

W/Cdr Sir John Hodsell, the Director General of Civil Defence training, visited Poole and had addressed the Council on the need for Civil Defence and, in 1950, the Poole Council dutifully complied. It re-appointed its Civil Defence Committee with Alderman A B Haynes as its enthusiastic Chairman. It appointed Jim O'Hara, the chief officer of the Dorset St John Ambulance Brigade, as its Training officer, and applied to be made the Scheme Making Authority, as it had been in the last years of the war.

Despite the energetic efforts of its Training Officer, there was little enthusiasm to volunteer for training in Civil Defence. No many more than 100 recruits had been enrolled by the end of the year, and an offer to pay the expenses of attendance at training sessions, and the award of a badge after ten hours' training did little to improve the situation. Nor was the Council any more successful in its application to be made a Scheme Making Authority. The Ministry replied that it would not make Poole a separate Scheme Making Authority unless it was found that a delegation agreement offered by the County Council was unsatisfactory. Then, the County Council went even further than Poole wanted in delegating responsibility for the whole of East Dorset, the Council was left to operate the scheme for East Dorset under the general aegis of the County Council.

The members of the Council were generally little more interested in Civil Defence than its townspeople. It seemed inconceivable that war could recur or that, if it did, anything effective could be done to mitigate the effects of atom bombs. So, while Ald Haynes and his officers pressed on gamely with their efforts to establish a trained Civil Defence force, members' main concern in the early part of 1950 was concentrated on the General Election.

The 1950 General Election was the first to be held for the newly constituted Poole constituency. It was therefore not clear what effect the loss of the votes of the rest of East Dorset would have on the result. Moreover, the Labour Party had found a strong candidate in Lt/Col Evelyn M King, who had been the MP for Penryn & Falmouth. Prior to the war he had been Headmaster of Clayesmore School at Blandford and he had been the Parliamentary Secretary to the Ministry of Housing & Town Planning in the Attlee Government. He had nursed the Poole Constituency for some time, and Clement Attlee had invited him to accompany him to open the new Poole Labour Party's Sports Ground at Fleets on the previous August Bank Holiday and, though a chill had stopped Mr Attlee fulfilling the engagement, Col King had come with Mrs Attlee and her daughter to open the grounds before a crowd of over 10,000 Poole people. The Poole Labour Party therefore felt that it had a good chance of upsetting the majority which Col Wheatley had obtained at the earlier East Dorset election.

The election proceedings prior to and during election day went well. There were no problems with the new Poole register of electors, now prepared by the Town Clerk, or the siting of the polling booths. It was, though, always thought that any problems that might arise would be from the very confined space of the Conference Room of the Municipal Buildings which allowed few counting assistants to be employed. It was therefore never anticipated that an early result would be able to be announced but, when a Presiding Officer and his ballot box was found to be missing, and only later found by the Police at his home in Merley with the ballot box in his car in the garage, the new constituency of Poole had the dubious distinction of being the last result to be declared that night!

Even so, as the Sheriff, the Mayor and the candidates went out on to the balcony of the Municipal Buildings at 3.45 am to announce the result they were greeted by an ironic cheer from the small crowd which had patiently waited in the forecourt of the buildings.

There had been a large poll. From an electorate of 56,606, the votes cast were as follows:

Major Mervyn Wheatley (Con)	24,344
Lt/Col Evelyn M King (Lab)	17,831
William Ridgeway (Lib)	6,531

Nationally, the Labour Party won 315, the Conservatives 298 with 9 for the Liberals and others. In his victory speech from the Municipal Buildings' balcony

Major Wheatley, having already heard the results of the other constituencies, warned his supporters to be ready for another early election.

To most people in Poole, it was no surprise that Major Wheatley was re-elected and there were no surprises in the Local elections that May. Of those who were to take a leading part in the proceedings of the Council on the Labour Party's behalf, 'Ron' Hart, the Vice Chairman of the Hamworthy Labour Party was elected for the Hamworthy Ward, and 'Charlie' Wells, for 12 years the Chairman of Poole Labour Party, was re-elected for the Newtown Ward. Nor was it any great surprise that Judith Hart, the Labour candidate in the Parkstone Ward, and destined to take a leading part in the affairs of the Labour Party in Parliament, and to end her Parliamentary career as Dame Judith Hart in the House of Lords, was defeated.

The real surprise to most people in Poole was the announcement in May that year that Major Wheatley, owing to the illness of his wife, would not be standing for Parliament at the subsequent election. He had, presumably, warned his local party, for a new prospective Conservative candidate was quickly announced. It was to be Captain Richard Pilkington MC. He had been Civil Lord of the Admiralty in Churchill's Coalition Government and the local Conservative party anticipated that he would be given a post in any future Conservative Government which was formed.

It was, too, that same month that the formal ceremony of admitting Olave, Lady Baden-Powell, to the Roll of Honorary Freemen of the Borough was held. Lady Olave was thought of as a local woman. As Olave St Clair Soames she had lived at 'Grey Rigg', Parkstone and had been educated at the school in St Osmund's Road. She had married General Baden-Powell at St Peter's, Parkstone, in 1912 and she told the Poole crowd which attended the ceremony, that she had first entered Scouting as Patroness of the Parkstone Boy Scouts' Troop.

Lady Baden-Powell was no ordinary person, and the ceremony of her admission was no ordinary one. On the day of the ceremony, she arrived from Brownsea Island in Commander Woollard's Girls' Sailing Ship, the 'Mary Rose', to a 'Peal of Welcome' from the bells of St James Church. The all-girl crew of the 'Mary Rose' landed her, rather precariously, at the Quay from which she was driven to Poole Park for the official ceremony which the band of the Royal Tank Regiment attended as well as the Girl Guides from all over the county, together with a 'Fairy Ring' of Brownies and the Cubs had a Grand Howl.

That day's ceremony was quite an historic one in many respects. Lady Baden-Powell was the first woman Freeman in the long history of Poole and Alderman A B Haynes, the Mayor, was attended by Miss Mary Llewellin, Poole's first woman Sheriff in its 700 year's history. It was also the only time when a man and wife had both been honoured with the Freedom of the Borough.

Top: Councillor CW Wells.

Bottom: Lady Baden Powell on the occasion of receiving the freedom of the borough.

Top: The erosion of Canford Cliffs shore.

Bottom: The sea defences, the promenade and cliffs put at an angle of repose and planted.

Top: Councillor WH Cole.

Bottom: Canford Cliffs Library today.

A little while later, the practical-minded Lady Baden-Powell returned the silver casket which had been presented to her to hold the illuminated scroll of her admission to the Roll of Freemen. She was to have the scroll framed and could find no other use for the casket which would, she though, be more use to the Corporation than to herself! The result was that the whole proceedings cost the Corporation only £174.

With so many of its projects held up, it was a trying year for the Council, but some progress had been made. It was, for instance, able to establish a new branch library at Canford Cliffs. The Parks Committee had agreed to transfer the old Branksome Park Estate lodge in Pine Cliff Road, which it had previously used as a cafe, to the Library Committee which it converted for use as a library for the people of Canford Cliffs and Branksome Park.

The Council, too, was able to convince the Ministry of the immediate necessity for sea defence works to be carried out on the sea frontage of St Ann's Hospital at Canford Cliffs. The sea had made inroads into the cliffs which had become in danger of further collapse and, even in those straitened times, the Council was able to persuade the Ministry that sea defence works were urgently required, and that sanction to borrow the necessary money should be given. The work consisted of cutting back the cliff to an 'angle of repose', and for a sea wall with a protective promenade and groynes to be built in from of the cliffs. (The Council, with an eye to the future, provided for a promenade which was wide enough to accommodate a future row of beach chalets.) The cost of the work was estimated at £30,000, towards which the Regional Hospital Authority agreed to contribute £10,000.

It was the Rector of Poole who instigated another small, but significant, development in the Old Town. He called upon the Council under the provisions of the Disused Burial Grounds Act, to take over responsibility for the old Hunger Hill Burial Ground which the church was no longer able to maintain. It was not a request which the Council could legally refuse but, in fact, the Council was only too ready to accept for the land would make a most convenient space for the Old Town. The tombstones were taken up and moved to the perimeter of the land after a careful note had been made of all the inscriptions which were still legible, and the land levelled and grassed for use as a public open space.

But the Council only grudgingly accepted the church graveyard. Rather than take it over, the Council first offered the Parochial Council a grant of £25 to continue to be responsible for the maintenance of the graveyard, but the Parochial Council was not tempted to withdraw its request, even though all that was then required was the repair of the perimeter wall. There was no reference, in this case, of noting the inscriptions of gravestones or of their removal so, presumably, the stones had already been removed. This was unfortunate as most

Top: The Municipal Buildings pre-war. *Bottom:* Hunger Hill open space today.

of the old worthies of Poole had been buried in the churchyard, and many of their epitaphs had been composed by the 'Poole Poet', Harry Price. Most of these epitaphs have been lost, which is a pity, judging by the epitaph which the 'Poole Poet' wrote ready for his own grave before his death in 1759, which was 'here lies the greatest of sinners, the least of the poets'!

The Parks Committee that year, though, had one great success. It was to obtain the Government's approval to taking over from the Roads & Engineering Committee its disused refuse tip at Whitecliff. The Council had been criticised for a long time over the condition of this old tip, especially by Councillor Cole, son of Harry Cole, who had been the firebrand of an earlier Council. At an earlier meeting of the Council, Councillor Cole had registered the complaints of nearby residents to the nuisance caused by the rotting refuse in dramatic form by majestically waving above his head a very large bottle of maggots which, he claimed, he had picked up from the tip on his way to the Council meeting.

The Parks Committee had the thought that the area would make a most convenient open space, and had persuaded the Council that the conversion of the refuse tip to an open space would make a lasting contribution to the Festival of Britain and, with the Festival being the Government's own brainchild, it was possible that a loan sanction might well be granted. But as it turned out, the cost of the work, which included a wall to prevent any seepage into the harbour, was greater than was first thought and the Ministry refused loan sanction for the £23,264 required. However, a deputation from the Council was finally able to persuade the Ministry to approve the scheme and even agree that the work could commence.

In fact, this success was not the only Ministerial refusal which succumbed to the persuasion of a deputation from the Council. The Council's long-term plan was to develop a Civic Centre round the existing Municipal Buildings and Police Station comprising all the land between Sandbanks Road and Commercial Road to the west of Park Road. In 1950 it so happened that the three properties which would be needed to complete the site of the Civic Centre, 'Seacombe', 2 Park Road; 'Brackendene' 2 Commercial Road and 'Courtenay Lodge', Sandbanks Road, were for sale, and, the Council contended, could be bought for £17,000. The Council's deputation argued that it was an opportunity which was unlikely to recur, and the town desperately needed a town hall, a central library and a swimming bath.

The members of the deputation were pleasantly surprised, a little later, to hear that they had succeeded in obtaining the Ministry's approval to raising a loan to buy the houses, and the committee wasted no time in completing the purchases, even though a Compulsory Purchase Order had to be made for one of the properties. Their acquisition provided most useful temporary accommodation for some sections of the staff to be moved from the Municipal Buildings which allowed members of the Council to re-occupy their two Committee rooms there for the first time since the beginning of the war.

But not all the Council's hopes for that year were realised. Despite all its efforts, there seemed nothing it could do to persuade Bournemouth Council seriously to consider activating the proposals of the Joint Drainage Committee. It had, though, at last succeeded in having one meeting of that Committee summoned, but when it met, all that had been agreed was to ask the Borough Engineers of the three authorities to make a report to it on whether the sewage could be treated chemically to render it innocuous before being discharge into the sea.

It was some months later that the Poole Council became aware of the contents of the Engineers' report. The three Engineers had reported that, not only had they found 'no method of purifying sewage chemically', and they had decided that there were no 'methods of improving the treatment of sewage with the present method of discharging it into the Bay'. They had agreed that there was no further enquiry or action which they could take, and that the question was now entirely one for the Joint Committee to consider.

At the meeting of the Poole Council, when the contents of the engineers' report were made known, and that the Bournemouth Council was unwilling to call a further meeting of the Joint Committee to consider it, there was, according to the local press, an 'Uproar of Resentment'. It was said that the Bournemouth Council considered that the cost of the joint scheme, originally estimated at £800,000, but then estimated at £2,250,000, was too great to contemplate, especially as the original agreement provided that Bournemouth would pay 80% of the total cost.

The Poole Council decided to take another tack. It resolved to invite the Bournemouth Branch of the British Medical Association to its subsequent meeting to discuss the problem. But the local doctors wisely decided not to be drawn on to one side of a high-profile local dispute. The Branch Secretary replied that the Association would rather make any representations they wished to make on the subject to the Joint Committee.

By December that year no further progress had been made and Councillor Lloyd-Allen proposed that the other two boroughs should be invited to appoint representatives to meet the Ministry of Health to ascertain its attitude to the problem. The Poole Council passed the motion unanimously, but it cut no ice with the Councils of Bournemouth or Christchurch. Both Councils refused to take part in any deputation, and the problem ended the year where it had begun!

The strange thing was that, during this time of tension between the local authorities, though apparently unperturbed about the disposal of sewage into the Bay, they were greatly concerned about the possible effect on their bathing beaches of fly ash from the Poole Generating Station being deposited out to sea.

No objections had been taken to an earlier application by the Electricity Board to the dumping of 100,000 cubic yards of mud, sand, clay and chalk dredged from Holes Bay for the foundations of the Generating Station, and the Board of Trade had detailed a specific area of sea where the Board's hoppers had deposited the spoil.

However, Bournemouth Council was very concerned as to the effect which the deposit of ash into the sea might have on its bathing beaches and called a meeting of representatives of the Poole and Christchurch Councils. The other two Councils shared the concern of Bournemouth and, after a number of joint meetings, it was agreed that all three Councils would oppose the proposal of the Electricity Board to dispose of ash out to sea 'with the utmost vigour'.

But, while this was going on, the Poole Council was having its own problems arising from the construction of the new Generating Station. When Alderman Langridge (known affectionately at the Municipal Offices as 'Sudan Sam' from his tales of his service in the Sudan as an engineer) had as Mayor, laid the foundation stone of the Generating Station in May, 1948, the Corporation had anticipated that it would receive a healthy boost to its rateable value as soon as the station became operational. However, with nationalisation, the Government had changed the rules. The amount of rates payable by nationalised public services, such as electricity and gas would, in future, it decided, be settled by the Government and, far from obtaining a boost to its rateable value, the town's rateable value was substantially reduced!

Nor was this the only problem caused to the Council by the nationalisation of the Old Bournemouth & Poole Electricity Company. Originally, when that company had proposed building the station, its output was thought only to satisfy the demands of the local communities. With nationalisation, a national grid was formed, whereby power was transmitted all round the country, connecting one power station with another, each contributing its output into the grid. With the new Poole station being connected to the national grid, it meant that lines of pylons had to be erected to carry cables to and from the new generating station. The Board was, therefore, in getting ready for the station to become operational, planning applications for the siting of these pylons.

These planning applications came as a shock to the Council. It had strong objection to many of the proposed sites for the pylons. The pylons would make, 'an unwarranted intrusion into amenities' of the districts in which they were planned. The high-tension cables, the Planning Committee decided, must be put underground.

The Committee's position, however, was untenable. The Board had a right of appeal to the Minister of Fuel & Power which had allowed such pylons in other parts of the country. To put the lines underground would cost a £1m a mile. The Council soon realised that more would be gained by negotiation as to the siting of the lines to do as little damage as possible to the town's amenities than in trying to enforce a refusal and, in this, it had some success. The Board promised, for instance, never to apply for three lines to be run parallel to each other; that no lines of cables would be laid alongside highways and that care would be exercised not to erect pylons on the skyline.

There were, in the process of agreeing the line of these pylons, many arguments. In a break from one of these arguments the Board's representatives raised its other problem, then being discussed in the local Press, of the disposal of the fly ash from the Board's new generating station. One of the Board's members mentioned that at one inland Power Station the local authority had accepted the ash from its local Power Station to reclaim derelict land. The ash had been found, he said, to be very good for this purpose for it readily absorbed water in wet weather and, in dry weather, water was attracted to the surface by the ash, and supported grass well on quite a thin cover of earth. He invited the Poole representatives to visit Reading to see the process in action.

It was only a few days later that Wilfrid Haskins, the Chairman of the Planning Committee and a leading horticulturalist of Coy Pond Nurseries, accompanied by officers of the Council, went to Reading to inspect the operation of land-recovery by the use of the ash.

On their return to Poole, the party reported how impressed they had been with the Reading operation, and that they had already found an appropriate area of land at Hamworthy. It was an area of about 100 acres which was boggy, lying below sea level and usually flooded and, though a small part of it was let for summer grazing, the Ministry of Agriculture & Fisheries would probably not object to a change of use, and an officer of the Southern Sea Fisheries had already agreed to raise no objection so long as he was satisfied that a sufficient bund would be built to ensure that ash could not escape into the harbour.

With the Council's agreement being obtained, it was then possible to come to an agreement with the Electricity Board. A great amount of water then drained on to the land from the hinterland which required no less than three 36-inch diameter pipes to drain it. The Board agreed to carry out this work and to take off what top soil there was so that it could later be placed on top of the ash filling, and to build a bund against the harbour frontage. It agreed that it would convey the ash from the Generating Station in covered trucks to ensure against spillage on the roads, and to tip the land with the ash to a depth of 16 feet.

There was no time to be wasted as the Generating Station was nearing completion. The Corporation made a compulsory purchase order in April for the purchase of 83 acres of land and made a loan application to borrow £1,500, being £1,000 for the land, £400 for fencing the land, and £100 for incidental costs. The ministry on this occasion needed little persuasion to grant the loan sanction and, within a few days of the Joint Committee's resolution to oppose

Top: Councillor Wilfrid Haskins.

Bottom: Turlin Moor Recreation Ground today.

the dumping of ash into the sea, the agreement between the Corporation and the Electricity authority had been executed. It was estimated that 53,000 tons of ash would be deposited each year and that, as from 1953, an area of about 7 acres would be reclaimed each year.

Considering the state of the country that year, the Corporation had done well. It failed in its attempt to have the huge oil tank removed from the Park near the Seldown entrance, despite threatening the Gas Board with a charge of £3 for every day it remained but, with the Gas Board asserting that it was necessary to retain it to hold gas oil before it was transported to its Bourne Valley works for treatment, the Committee relented for, with the electricity supplies unable to meet the demand, gas supply had become even more important.

There was, however, still one other notable success that year. The Council, to its great satisfaction, was told that its application for the return of its Commission of the Peace was successful. Poole's Magistrates Court and its Quarter Sessions were saved from their threatened transfer to the County Council. But that did not free it from other provisions of the Justices of the Peace Act, 1949. In future Mayors of Poole would no longer automatically become the Chairmen of the Poole Bench of Magistrates and, though the Mayor would still be a Justice during the time of his mayoralty, he would cease to be a Magistrate for the following year as had been the case earlier.

The logo of the Festival of Britain.

1951

THE FESTIVAL OF GREAT BRITAIN

'It is like 1940 without the bombing and casualties, – but also without the sense of national unity.'

(Harold Macmillan, Oct.1951)

1950 had been a turbulent year of strikes, rationing and shortages. The fear of bombing raids had gone but, otherwise, conditions of life were little different from wartime.

But, for all that, the Government, despite criticism of it being an 'ill-timed frivolity', had decided that there would be a nationwide celebration in 1951, a 'Festival of Britain', to mark the centenary of the Great Exhibition. The centrepiece of the Festival was an exhibition to celebrate Britain's achievements in 'Power and Production, Sea and Ships' to be housed on an area of 27 acres on the South Bank of the Thames between Westminster and Waterloo Bridges, an area which had been 'Blitzed' in the war, and all the towns of Britain had been invited to celebrate the centenary in their towns.

But 1951 did not live up to the high hopes implied by these proposed celebrations. The year began with the meat ration being reduced to 8d (3p) a week, the lowest it had ever been; a ration which gave each ration-book holder the equivalent to one small mutton chop per week!

Nor did Hugh Gaitskell's Budget of early April induce a spirit of festival. Defence costs had escalated as the Korean War had intensified, and the cost of the National Health Service had risen alarmingly. The new Chancellor claimed that he had spread the new burdens widely and thinly. Tax increases were certainly widespread. Income Tax was increased by 6d (2.5p) to make the standard rate 9/6d (47.5p) in the £; the petrol tax was increased by 4.5d (2p); car tax and the purchase tax on household goods doubled, and profits distributed by companies were taxed at 50%. In addition, to try to bring the cost of the

National Health Service under control, patients were, in future, to pay for half the cost of spectacles and false teeth which were supplied by the Health Service.

The Government, however, had not allowed the worsened financial situation to impede the progress of its South Bank Exhibition. It was completed in early 1951 at a cost of £11m and it seemed destined to be successful as nearly 100,000 people visited it on its opening day in May.

The Poole Council was less enthusiastic. It had provided no money in its estimates to celebrate the event, apart from £100 for the ceremony of Beating the Bounds of the Harbour. But it did promise to make available the parks or premises required, and it encouraged the formation of a Festival Committee, made up of members of the public under the Chairmanship of Councillor Leslie Miller, which organised a Drumhead Service in Poole Park to begin the celebrations, and which included a Carnival, an 'Olde World Fayre', an Old Time Ball (in the newly constructed hall of Herbert Carter School), and the Youth Clubs of the borough arranged many sporting events.

The Council prided itself that no ratepayers' money was spent on the Festival celebrations, but it did decorate the Municipal Buildings with flags and bunting and it illuminated the Municipal Buildings at night. The Admiralty also helped by sending HMS Mandate and three minesweepers to the port during the fortnight of the celebrations, and the crews of the ships took part in the sporting events, and Carter's Pottery presented a specially-designed, commemorative vase to the Corporation for exhibition in the Mayor's Parlour.

But for all the festivities, there was no disguising the harshness of the time. Since the war the Government had induced periods of recession to counter-balance earlier periods of 'over-heating' which had brought serious inflation. This led to a 'Stop-Go' policy which made it impossible for the Council to plan its staff levels or its capital works programme with any confidence.

The new tight restrictions on capital spending in 1951 even affected the Council's one contribution to the Festival Year in the conversion of the old Whitecliff refuse tip into an open space. The Ministry in approving the scheme had only approved a loan for Part I of the work. The Council assumed then that its loan approval for Part II would be a mere formality. However, Festival or not, the Ministry was adamant, Part II had to be deferred.

It was the same answer to the Council's request for loan sanction for the building of its proposed new pumping station at Sturminster Marshall, the building of a new reservoir and laying of mains to supply Lytchett. These were deferred, and the proposal to install a softening plant for the water from Sturminster Marshall in the same way as the Corporation softened the water supplied from its Corfe Mullen works, was categorically refused as being unnecessary. The Council had other rebuffs that year, one of the most annoying

Top: Councillor Leslie Miller.

Bottom: Carter's commemorative vase.

being the Ministry's deferment of approvals for the Council to bring more of the town's gravelled roads up to an acceptable standard.

It is, perhaps, not surprising that the Government had to adopt such draconian measures, for inflation since the war had already halved the value of the pound and had had a serious effect on the Corporation's costs. Wages, as well as the cost of all materials, had risen sharply, and builders of Council houses had already been demanding substantial additional payments to cover the extra costs. As early as January that year the Council had no option but to agree an extra payment of £30,000 in the case of a contract to build houses in Hamilton Road, and £46,455 in respect of houses built on the Trinidad Estate. What was more, it had then become impossible to find builders willing to tender to build houses within the Government's limit of 30/- per superficial foot.

To mitigate the mounting costs of house building, the Government once again reduced the specification of Council houses. From an earlier minimum standard of 1000 sq ft for council houses, the ministry suggested that the size of rooms might be reduced to allow 3-bedroomed houses to be built containing only 900 superficial feet, and 2-bedroomed houses to contain a total of only 750 sq ft. But, although the Council adopted some of these reduced standards which brought an estimated saving of between £30 and £80 a house, the cost per sq ft was, if anything, increased, and the ministry had no option but to agree to the Council's urgent request that its cost limit of 35/- per sq ft should be increased.

With the increase in the price of building, the Council decided that it was only equitable for the controlled selling price of private houses which had been built under licence, to be increased. This gave a new maximum selling price for a house in Evering Avenue which had then recently been built of £1,350, and a house, built some two years earlier in Herm Road, of £1,200!

But it was not only the cost of building which was of concern to the Estates Committee. To obtain areas of land of sufficient size for new housing estates, the committee was having to go into the more northern, unsewered areas of the town. It had then purchased a large area north of Sopers Lane which it had already christened 'the Waterloo Estate'. This area of land was near to the Broadstone sewage works, but those works were already so inadequate that a party of Germans, invited that year by the Foreign Office to study local government in England, happily were unaware that hidden below the flood water which they saw on their journey to Broadstone, lay the then completely submerged Broadstone Sewage Works!

In fact, though, the Estates Committee had never assumed, in choosing the Waterloo estate, that it could be drained into the Broadstone Works. It had assumed that the negotiations, begun some years earlier with the Wareham & Purbeck Council, to sewer Upton and Hamworthy jointly to new sewage works

Top: Builders' advertisement 1951–52.

Bottom: Council houses built in 1951.

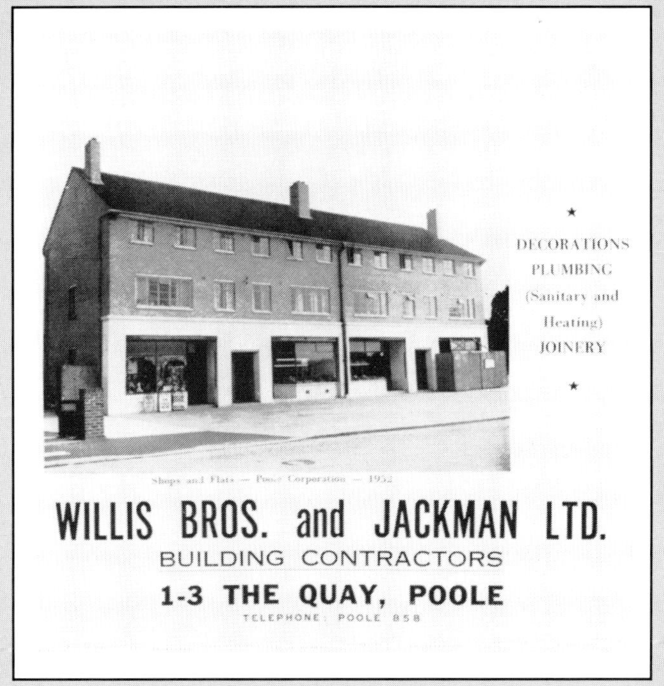

which the Corporation was to build on Turlin Moor at Hamworthy, would be concluded and that the new works would be completed in time for it to take the drainage of the Waterloo Estate. However, in 1951, negotiations broke down over a dispute with the Rural District Council as to the likely final population of Upton on which the apportionment of the costs of building the Works was to be calculated. The Estate Committee, with the breakdown of the negotiations, suddenly faced the dire prospect of having houses completed on the Waterloo Estate without a system of drainage being available for their drainage.

Councillor Lloyd-Allen proposed that the council should pull out of the Joint Drainage Committee with Bournemouth and Christchurch so that Poole could be free to make its own plans, but Alderman Reeves reported that the Bournemouth Labour Party had already asked the Minister of Local Government & Planning to institute a Public Inquiry 'into the serious sewerage problem of Bournemouth, Poole and Christchurch and the resulting condition of Poole Bay, owing to the failure of the Bournemouth Council to take any effective action, despite representations of neighbouring authorities', and the Council agreed to defer any decision on Councillor Lloyd-Allen's motion to await a decision by the Minister. The report of this meeting of the Poole Council in the Press at least brought the matter to a head. Lt/Col Turner of Bournemouth retorted that it was the Poole Council which was primarily responsible for the work not having been proceeded with before the war. Councillor Lloyd Allen replied with Poole's version of the history of the Joint Committee's proceedings since 1935, purporting to show that it had always been the Poole Council which had wished to expedite the scheme.

Whatever the pros and cons of the matter, it was quite clear that, failing anything which the Minister could do, there was no hope of the pre-war joint scheme ever being implemented.

The Minister, meanwhile, had responded to the request of the Bournemouth Labour Party by calling a meeting of the representatives of the three towns in Whitehall. He had no power to instruct Councils what they should do, but he did the next best thing, he called on the three Councils to inform his Ministry what their future plans were to deal with the sewage of their boroughs.

It was not until April, 1952, that the Poole Council was informed that the Bournemouth Council had told the Minister that it had already agreed to install a new maceration plant on its existing system, had agreed a combined drainage plan for Winton, and was considering a scheme to drain back some sewage to a proposed new works at Holdenhurst. The Christchurch Council had informed the Minister that it was working on a scheme to divert all its sewage to an inland works.

But the Poole Council had taken action in 1951. Immediately after the meeting with the Minister, the Council had instructed the Borough Engineer to produce 'a scheme for the interception and inland treatment of all the town's sewage'. It was an instruction which the Borough Engineer had anticipated. He had already prepared plans for the first stage of the scheme, comprising the rebuilding and enlargement of the Broadstone works at a cost of £154,370, which would be able to take the drainage of the Waterloo Estate. The plans were approved by Council and submitted for loan sanction within a few weeks of the meeting with the Minister who acted promptly enough for a Public Inquiry into the Council's application in October, 1951.

The prospect of a new Broadstone Works providing facilities for the drainage of the Waterloo Estate, at least solved the immediate problem of Geoffrey Bravery, the Chairman of the Estates Committee, and it was he, in his private capacity, who solved another of the Council's problems that year.

Clifford Brewer, a builder who had earlier himself been a Councillor, had been granted a 7-year licence to use the Poole Stadium to operate Speedway Racing. The fee had been agreed at £1000 a year, but the Speedway had not proved a financial success and, in 1951, Mr Brewer had applied for a reduction of the rent. He had, he stated, made a loss that year and anticipated a further loss in the following season. He suggested that the rent should be reduced to £400. The Council was only willing to make a small reduction and, when it became impossible to come to an agreement, the Council cancelled the licence and advertised for new offers to operate the concession.

As a result of the advertisement, the Council received only two offers. A partnership of three local men offered £1250 a year; a partnership consisting of Councillors Bravery and Matchan offered £850 a year with an additional percentage of receipts which could, in favourable circumstances, bring their rent up to £1500. The Council accepted the first offer of £1250 but, before the agreement was executed, the offer was withdrawn, and the Council was left with only the offer of the two councillors. With the opening of the racing season approaching, the Council accepted the offer of the two councillors.

The two new co-promoters of the Poole Speedway made an unlikely partnership. Councillor Leonard Matchan was a bespectacled, ebullient Socialist; a prosperous business man who had brought the manufacture of Max Factor cosmetics to a factory on the borders of Poole and his colleague, Ted Webster, an engineer, came from London to establish an adjoining factory to manufacture lipstick cases. Councillor Geoffrey Bravery, the operator of the three cinemas in Poole and one in Commercial Road, Bournemouth, was, on the other hand, a fervent Conservative and Chairman of the local Party.

The licence to the partners, however, was not a controversial one, and neither of them were opposed in the local elections that year. in fact, only four seats were contested that year, which left the political balance of the Council unchanged, at 28 Conservative members, 8 Labour, 3 Liberal and one Independent.

Top: Councillor Leonard Matchan.

Bottom: Speedway 1952.

It was that year, too, when two members and one officer received honours. Councillor Lt/Cdr 'Tom' Sherrin, who had been elected to the Council in 1949 after distinguished war service in the navy, and who had been a notable swimmer and water polo player, was awarded the OBE for his services to the Sea Cadets. Alderman 'Fred' Reeves, who had earlier been awarded the Military Medal in the service of the Wiltshire Regiment in the First World War, was awarded the OBE for political services, and Morgan Phillips, the Secretary of the Labour Party, also honoured him by coming to Poole to present him with a cheque to mark his 27 years' service to the Labour Party.

But, though there had been no change in the composition of the Council, there were many changes that year in the senior staff of the Council. Dr George Chesney, Poole's Medical Officer of Health, retired after 21 years' service to the Corporation, and was succeeded by Dr James Hutton. Dr Chesney, at the instance of the Ministry of Health, was awarded the OBE for his researches into diphtheria immunisation. T J B Price, the Deputy Borough Engineer, a qualified architect, also retired that year to be succeeded by Lt/Col 'Bob' Hawker, a local man, already the holder an OBE from his service in the Army during the war, and then an engineer with Brighton Corporation. John Wallace, then the only other solicitor after the Town Clerk and Deputy, resigned to enter private practice, and was replaced by T M H Scott, a solicitor from Burton Upon Trent (who later became Town Clerk of Finchley). Another event affecting the management of the Council affairs for a little time that year was the serious car accident in which Wilson Kenyon, the Town Clerk, was involved.

It was, though, a surprise to some people in Poole at the time that Alderman 'Joe' Bright had not joined the other members of the Council in being awarded some honour in view of his unprecedented length of service as Mayor of Poole all through the war years. However, if Alderman Bright was disappointed, he did not show it or reduce his endeavours, as Chairman of the Parks Committee, to improve and increase the area of Poole's parks, open spaces and amenities.

In fact, an opportunity to increase the area of public open space occurred that year. Some four years earlier, the Council had zoned an area of 8 acres in Branksea Avenue, adjoining Hamworthy Park, for the Establishment of a holiday camping site. With the Government's severe restrictions on the purchase of foreign currency, holidays abroad were almost impossible. To meet the demand for holidays in Britain holiday caravan camps had been established all over the country, especially in Dorset, to provide reasonably cheap, self-catering holidays and it was to provide such a camp that the Council had zoned the site in Hamworthy for this purpose. But, in 1951, the Council was persuaded that there was a better site further west on Ham Common, and this gave the Parks Committee the opportunity to have the Branksea Avenue site zoned for an extension of Hamworthy Park.

The newly agreed holiday camping site was an area fronting the harbour, south of the war-time 'HMS Turtle' on Ham Common. HMS Turtle comprised the northern half of Ham Common which was all owned by Lord Rockley. HMS Turtle occupied an area of some 100 acres laying alongside the railway line to Weymouth, and was an area of land which the Estates Committee had long coveted for development as a Council housing estate but, as the land was still under requisition by the Admiralty, no compulsory purchase order could be made to acquire it without Admiralty agreement. The Council had mounted a deputation to the Admiralty as early as 1945 to ask it to derequisition the land. That deputation had had no success but, as the land remained derelict and unoccupied, the Council had each year renewed its request for the land's release. It had enlisted the help of the town's MP and even the ministry itself, but the Admiralty had been unmoved. The land it decided, had to be retained.

However, during these years, the members of the Council and its officers had become familiar with a further large area of Ham Common which lay to the south of the Admiralty land which had a frontage of nearly a mile to the harbour. At that time the main area of the southern part of the land could only be approached by a farm track leading through the Admiralty's land, but there was a steep track leading off Napier Drive alongside the disused Doulton's clay pit to the pier from which aviation fuel had been pumped to the tanks built into the hillside from which it was run into petrol tankers on the railway line behind to provide fuel for the RAF airfields in Dorset. The deep, disused claypit had become flooded, and it had seemed to the Committee that it would form a pleasant centre-piece for a holiday caravan camping site to be built around it. It was therefore decided to zone an area of 50 acres round the lake formed in the clay pit for the establishment of a holiday camping site.

It so happened that it was then easy to change the planned zoning to allow for the holiday camp for it was that year that the County Planning Officer at last submitted the draft development Plan for Poole to the Council for its observations.

The draft plan did not include any proposals for the Old Town of Poole. The draft Written Statement accompanying the Plan merely stated that consideration of the planning of the Old Town had been deferred and that a Comprehensive Development Plan for the area would be submitted later. That was disappointing, for the Council had also received that year the recommendations of the Royal Commission on Historical Monuments. Its officers had spent a year inspecting the buildings of the Old Town and had recommended that the Ministry should schedule 253 of them as buildings of architectural or historical interest. The members of the Council reacted strongly, for if anything like this number of buildings was to be retained, their plans for the redevelopment of Old Poole would be seriously jeopardised. The Council complained to the Minister,

Top: Councillor 'Tom' Sherrin.

Bottom: Rockley Pier today.

asserting that most of the listed buildings were of little importance, most included only for a small detail in their construction, and that most of them were in no condition to be retained. There was, however, nothing further the Council could do, pending the preparation of the redevelopment plan for the Old Town.

The Council had few strong views about the content of the Draft Plan itself for, in fact, it had been produced in close consultation with the Council's own officers. The members realised, too, the difficulty of producing a blue-print of how a town should be developed over the following twenty years. This was especially so in the case of a town such as Poole which had grown so unexpectedly quickly in the previous twenty years. In fact, the provisional figures for the Census which had been taken that April showed that Poole's population, despite over five years of war, had grown at a rate of more than 1000 a year. Its population had risen from 60,196 in 1931 to 82,958 in April that year.

The Council, however, strongly objected to the County Council's estimate of Poole's population as reaching 96,000 in 1971. The Council's own officers had considered that the likely population of Poole in 1971 was 103,000 and the Committee's first thoughts were that the estimated figure was being suppressed by the County to show the likely population in 1971 as being less than 100,000, a figure often referred to as a likely minimum for a town to be granted County Borough status. The Council finally got its way by having the estimate amended to 103,000.

The Council's only other quarrel with the draft plan was the area of land zoned for industrial development. Sir Patrick Abercrombie, in his plan, had provided for a doubling of Poole's industry but, even while the present Development Plan was being considered, the Board of Trade had written to the Council, specifically warning that it would grant few, if any, of its Certificates permitting the erection of industrial buildings in Poole. It had stated that these Certificates were granted on the basis of the unemployment in the particular area in which the proposed building was to be situated. In the case of Poole, the Board had asserted, the degree of unemployment was negligible and, in the Boards' view, it was likely to remain so. It was therefore very unlikely that any certificates to allow further industrial buildings in Poole would be granted except, perhaps, for the extension of existing industries. It strongly advised the Council to agree to little land being zoned in the Borough for industrial use.

The Council resisted what they considered to be a political restraint being enshrined in a Development Plan, designed to last for twenty years, and the County Planning Officer was persuaded to provide for at least a reasonable amount of industrial development on the ground that the definition of 'industrial' in the Town Planning Acts included warehousing, which did not need the Board Of Trade Certificate, and that provision of a considerable area for

Top: The Ryvita Factory today. *Bottom:* The South Western Pottery.

Top: The South Western Pottery. *Bottom:* The Herbert Carter School today.

industrial development would be required for the relocation of industries from residential areas.

At the time, industry generally was having a difficult time and its prospects for the following year were not encouraging with the Government demanded a saving of between 20% and 30% of industry's normal use of fuel that autumn and winter.

But, despite everything, Poole industries seemed to be doing well. The new, large 'garage' building erected for the Humphris company between Ringwood Road and Old Wareham Road was rapidly being converted into a factory for the Ryvita Company. Christopher Hill's new premises on the Quay were opened that year. Chalwyn Lamps, British Seagull, British Diamond Wire all extended their accommodation. Hamworthy Engineering stated that it was doing as much business in a month as it did in a year before the war, and was building an extra fitting shop at its premises on the Hamworthy Quay and the huge Pitwines Gasworks was producing 21,000,000 cubic feet of gas a day.

Already, too, the problems of industrial use in residential areas had arisen. Loewy Engineering Company, a designer of rolling mills and hydraulic presses, had moved from London twelve years earlier, to carry on its business at 'Branksome Grange', a large house in St Aldhem's Road, Branksome. In 1951 it applied for planning permission to extend its premises, and officers visiting the company in connection with the application, found that the company was also using two large premises nearby in Lindsay Road. The Council refused the planning application and threatened proceedings in regard to the unauthorised use of the two large houses in Lindsay Road. The upshot of the matter was that the company agreed to move its whole operation to new premises to be built in Wallisdown Road, Poole, and, with the support of the Council, the Board of Trade was persuaded to grant its Certificate to allow the relocation of the business to the new buildings to be erected there, no doubt influenced by the importance of the firm and the country's engineering and aluminium industries. The death of the founder of the firm in 1942 had been described as the equivalent of the loss of an Army Corps.

As for the Council's own capital projects that year, they were confined to the completion of projects begun earlier. Properties in Commercial Road near Ashley Cross were purchased for a future widening of the A35. The Herbert Carter Secondary School was formally opened, and the Sylvan Road School was completed. The only new projects that year were confined to the urgent problems of sea defence works for which loan sanction was likely. A scheme for the protection of properties at Sandbanks as well as the harbour frontage at Pearce Avenue were completed and a scheme to protect the sea frontage of the old Canford Cliffs Hotel was agreed with the owners.

But, though the Council's own activities were constrained, it became very involved with plans which were being made by the Ministry of Agriculture & Food to rectify the overcrowded conditions at its abattoir at Bushell Mill farm as well as the Ministry of Health's proposal to build a new hospital to supplant Poole's Cornelia Hospital.

The Ministry had been impressed by the Corporation's complaint of the poor facilities at Bushell Mill Farm to deal adequately with the large number of animals slaughtered and of the difficulties experienced by the Sanitary Inspectors in their inspection of the meat produced. The Ministry had finally agreed that year that new facilities were urgently required. It was, though, not easy to agree where a new abattoir should be built. The Ministry's first proposal was to build its new slaughter-house at a site near to the Hamworthy Junction, a site which the Council opposed. The Ministry's second suggestion was that the new premises should be built on the site of the existing abattoir. The Council felt that this would inhibit the development of the surrounding area, and was able to claim it did not comply with the draft development plan. The Council was finally relieved to be told that the Ministry had agreed a site at Uddens Cross in the Wimborne district.

The Ministry of Health also had its problems in deciding on the site for its proposed new hospital. Its officials suggested a number of alternative sites, some outside Poole, but seemed to favour a site near the Wallisdown Road. There were some, including Poole's Medical Officer of Health, who preferred the site of the Corporation's old Infectious Diseases' Hospital in Ringwood Road, Alderney. But the Council, through Councillor Bravery, the Chairman for the Poole Hospital's Management Committee, pressed for the new hospital to be built on the site of the existing Cornelia Hospital. However, no decision had been made before Parliament was dissolved and the matter was deferred until a new Government was formed.

Councillor Matchan was chosen as the Labour candidate for the General Election which was called for 25th October that year. Leonard Matchan, as might have been expected, put up a rumbustious campaign, touring the streets of the town in his Jaguar car fitted with a most effective loud speaker on the roof. But it was of little avail. Though he increased the Labour vote by 500, Poole's new Conservative candidate, Capt Richard Pilkington, increased the Conservative vote by over 2500. The vote of the unfortunate William Ridgway, again the Liberal candidate, was squeezed by the two larger parties. His vote was down by some 1500, and he lost his deposit. The result was:

Capt Richard Pilkington	26,998
Leonard Matchan	18,346
William Ridgway	5,029

The Conservatives' campaign of 'Set the People Free' and their promise to abolish rationing, had won them a majority of 17, and Churchill again became Prime Minister, once again at a difficult time. Harold Macmillan was appointed Minister of Local Government and Housing with the task of inspiring local authorities and private builders to produce 300,000 houses a year, a figure which had never before been achieved. On taking office, he said, 'it is like 1940 without the bombing and casualties – but also without the sense of national unity!'

Major Wheatley, who had retired from Parliament at its dissolution, had served Poole well. He had also been assiduous in his attendance at the House in which he had acted as the Whip to the Conservative party in opposition. In the New Year's Honours list of 1952 he was to be created a knight Bachelor.

The year ended with the Poole Council still 'full of itself'. Its pride and hopes for the future had been given a boost in the year by the Select Committee of the House of Commons which had been established to recommend what functions should be transferred to the county councils. It had recommended that the Weights and Measures services of non-county boroughs should be transferred to the county councils except for the towns of Cambridge, Luton and Poole. These towns should, exceptionally, retain these duties, it recommeded.

It was time, the Council decided, with the appointment of a new Postmaster General, to make another attempt to persuade him to give all districts of the town a 'Poole' postal address. Lord Llewellin was asked to make an appointment for a deputation to see the new Postmaster General to put its case.

Nor had the Council lost its appetite to become a County Borough. Surely, it was thought, the new Government would at last tackle the long-delayed problem of the boundaries and powers of local government and to be ready for such an eventuality, the Council asked 'Bill' Julyan, the Borough Treasurer, to prepare financial statistics showing what the likely financial effect would be of Poole Council attaining County Borough status.

Other plans for the future which were made that year were, however, not inspired by the Council, but by the people of Poole. A group of Poole people decided that Poole would hold its own Festival in 1952, celebrating the long history of Poole. This decision was made even while the Festival Committee was still busy organising Poole's contribution to the Festival of Britain.

The idea of a Pageant of Poole might have been inspired by the appearance of the first volume of H P Smith's 'History of the Town and County of Poole' that year. The Council had earlier sponsored the History by agreeing to buy 2000 copies for the use in schools, and by the then recent publication of a book of memoirs by Herbert Carter which he had entitled 'I Call to Mind'. But, whatever had inspired the thought, it had been enthusiastically agreed to celebrate Poole's history in 1952 by a 'Pageant of Poole'.

Cover of Herbert Carter's *I Call to Mind.*

The Council readily agreed to make facilities available in Poole Park for the Pageant, but no financial commitments were made or requested. In fact, the enthusiastic promoters of the Pageant expected to make a profit and they had already decided to donate the proceeds to the Disabled Sailors' and Soldiers' Aid Society and, with Sir Mervyn Wheatley as Chairman of the Committee, and with the Earl of Shaftesbury as its president, and with the Mayors of Poole and Bournemouth, Lord Lyle, Lord Llewellin, Lord Rockley, Captain Pilkington and Viscount Cranborne as its patrons, everything seemed set fair for the Pageant to be a success!

The Corporation's loyal address.

1952

THE NEW ELIZABETHAN AGE

'Poole Old Town is about as impregnable to road traffic as an ancient walled town'.

(Poole Herald, May, 1952)

The second Elizabethan age began on 5th February with the sudden death of George VI at Sandringham. Princess Elizabeth, then in Kenya, was proclaimed Queen in London that same day. The following morning the Mayor proclaimed Elizabeth's accession from the balcony of the Municipal Buildings, accompanied by the Rector of Poole and the Aldermen and Councillors in their robes. Below, in the forecourt, school children had been assembled, and members of the public filled the nearby pavements, attracted by the playing of the band of the Royal Tank Regiment which completed the formalities by playing 'God Save the Queen'.

The Council went on to hold a meeting to agree a Loyal Address to be presented to the new Queen. Ever since the town had been made a County Borough by Elizabeth I, the Council had regularly memorialised the eighteen kings and queens who had succeeded her, either in congratulation or in sympathy, and the practice had continued ever since, even though the Council's powers had derived from Parliament, rather than the monarch, since the Corporations Act, 1835.

The Corporation's Loyal Address followed the form of previous memorials:

'To her Most Gracious Majesty Queen Elizabeth the Second by the Grace of God Queen of this Realm and of all her other realms and territories, Head of the Commonwealth, Defender of the Faith

May it please your Majesty:

We, your Majesty's most faithful and loyal subjects, the Mayor, Aldermen and Burgesses of the Town & County of the Borough of Poole, with all humble affection, approach the Throne, to offer to your Majesty our deep and sincere sympathy in the death of our late Revered Sovereign Lord, King George, of blessed and glorious memory . . .

The Council offer your Majesty their assurance of unswerving and deep affection . . . and wish you may long reign over a happy and contented people to the welfare of all your Majesty's loving subjects.'

The newspapers made much of the hopes that, with the Queen's accession, a new and glorious 'Elizabethan Age' would dawn. But the auguries were not good. R A Butler, the Chancellor of the Exchequer, was to announce that the sterling area was then 'in deficit all round the world', and that Britain was 'in danger of being bankrupt, idle and hungry'. Churchill, a little later, was to complain that 'Labour's Defence Programme was utterly beyond the nation's capacity to bear'.

It was hardly a situation in which much could be done to redeem the Conservatives' promise to 'Set the People Free', but some token changes were quickly made. Identity Cards were abolished; the Utility Mark which, since 1941, had dictated standards for such things as clothing and furniture, was scrapped, and the amount which householders could spend on the repair and maintenance of their houses was raised to £200 a year.

The Budget, though, reflected the country's financial predicament. Hire purchases were restricted, the yearly allowance of foreign currency which could be obtained for foreign travel was reduced to £25 a year, and it was announced that all Government expenditures were to be cut.

It was only too easy for the Government to cut local government expenditure. Its Ministry had already informed the Council that even such projects as the completion of the Whitecliff reclamation and the new pumping station at Sturminster Marshall, both of which had been previously approved by the Ministry, were to be deferred, and other schemes, such as changing rooms at Ladies Walking Field, new greenhouses at Poole Park and the erection of twelve new bus shelters, had already been rejected.

These deferments and refusals were bad enough, but the position in regard to the building of 150 houses at Waterloo had become quite desperate in early 1952. If the contracts for the erection of these houses were not executed before the end of the financial year in April, the Ministry's sanction to borrow the necessary money became automatically cancelled and the scheme took its chance with other Councils' applications in the following year. The Council's dilemma arose from the fact that the new houses at Waterloo needed the newly constructed Broadstone Sewage Works to be operational before the houses could be occupied, and the Ministry had still not then given its sanction to borrow the money.

The Council pressed the Ministry for formal loan sanction for the Broadstone Works. After all, the Council complained, the Ministry had held its Public Inquiry the previous autumn, and knew how urgent the work was, but had still not issued its formal approval. Despite urgent appeals, the Council could get no satisfaction. It was only when the Council appealed to Captain Pilkington, its Member of Parliament, to raise the matter in the House of Commons that a reply was forthcoming. The loan for the new Works would be approved in the next financial year, the Ministry wrote, but the Council was not to invite tenders for the work until after April, after the formal approval had been issued. This, at least, had been enough assurance for the council immediately to complete the building contracts for the Waterloo houses.

Poole, though, felt the effect of the Governments' restrictions on capital spending more than many other Councils, in that Poole had started the post-war period already seriously behind hand in the provision of schools. That year the Trinidad Primary School was completed, but it was only the third new school to have been built since the war. The lack of school places in the developing areas of the town was severe, made worse each year by the increasing population and by the drift of families from the Old Town into the newly developing areas of the town.

But at least there was a safety valve. With the drift of population out of the Old Town, the number of pupils attending schools in the Old Town had fallen quite dramatically, leaving room there for many more scholars. The Committee hired buses to take children into and out of the Old Town. The infants were taken to Lagland School, the juniors to South Road School and the seniors to Herbert Carter School. T L Higham, the Poole Education Officer, wrote to the parents concerned, assuring them that the three schools in the Old Town were very good schools. 'Indeed,' he wrote, 'they are among the best schools in Poole, and you need have no fear about the effect of transferring your children from whatever school they attend at present'.

But there was no such stop-gap arrangement possible in the case of the hundreds of unmade-up roads of the borough. These 'builders' gravelled roads were rapidly deteriorating even further with the increased motor traffic. Many, without surface-water drainage and without street lighting, had become dangerously rutted, and so became seriously flooded in wet weather. But the Ministry

Top: TL Higham Borough Education Officer.

Bottom: Poole Gasworks.

was quite adamant: loan sanction would never be given on the grounds of inconvenience or the deteriorating condition of roads. The only applications which would be considered were for individual roads, the making-up of which was essential on public health grounds.

It was, though, not only in unmade-up roads that street lighting was a problem in Poole. Most of Poole's made-up roads were then lit by gas and though it was said in 1834, when Poole had its first gas lamps, that people from all round the area came to Poole to marvel at the brilliance of the new gas lamps, in 1952, the dim pool of light which they cast seemed little use to pedestrians and none at all to motorists. Their light was insufficient even for the Superintendent of Police to give his 'certificate of exemption' to allow cars to be parked at night without lights in any of the streets of the borough.

The whole question of street lighting was raised in 1952 by the Gas Board demanding an increase in the price of gas. Its proposed new tariff raised the cost of gas consumed in the town's 3,200 gas lamps by £1850 a year. In informing the council of the increase the Gas Board also told the Council that the lamps needed to be fitted with automatic igniters at a cost of a further £3200, and each lamp, it informed the council, would then need a clock to control the igniters. The Board offered to hire the clocks to the Corporation for an annual charge of £950.

The Roads & Engineering Committee was taken aback by these demands. Its long-term policy was to convert all street lamps to electricity. It already had 273 electric lamps, mainly those recently erected in the new housing estates, which were maintained by the Electricity Board, and it had 473 bollards and traffic signs using electricity which the Borough Engineer's Department had installed and maintained.

The Committee asked the Borough Engineer to estimate what it would cost for the Corporation to take over responsibility for the whole of the lighting of the borough, and asked for inquiries to be made as to the likelihood of a loan sanction being granted to convert all street lights to using electricity. The Borough Engineer's estimate for maintaining the existing lamps was £14,000, but the Committee was told that there was no chance whatsoever of loan sanction being granted for a general conversion scheme.

The Committee decided that, as from April, 1953, the Corporation would take over the responsibility for the street lighting of the borough and, as it seemed inevitable that Poole had to put up with its gas lights for some time to come, the Committee agreed that the Gas Board should fit the automatic lighters to the gas lamps and that twelve of the board's employees would be taken over by the Corporation to carry out the maintenance.

The Committee decided, however, that a special case had to be made in respect of the existing electrically operated lights in the main roads of the

Miss Llewellin, Mayor.

borough. The standards on which these lights had been mounted were the old iron pillars which had been erected by the old Poole Tramway Company in 1902 to support the tram wires. In 1935, when the buses had replaced the trams in Poole, the pillars had been retained and street lights attached to them. They were not well positioned to light the roads but, worst of all, the hollow shafts had, over the years, gradually rusted from the inside and had become dangerous. Two had collapsed into the road, and one of them had killed a boy who had been walking in the street. Even in those poverty-stricken days, the Committee felt that the Ministry must approve their urgent replacement. It instructed that an application be made for the sanction to borrow £5,000 so that concrete lamp-posts could be substituted for the metal ones.

The Gas Board's claim for extra money was, however, only one of a multitude of increased prices. Electricity charges, bus fares, building materials, wages and salaries were all increased, and the rise in interest rates alone was estimated to cost the Corporation an extra £6000 a year.

The members of the Council were alarmed at the effect that these increases would have on the Council's own rate demand for, with losing rateable value with the new system of calculating the amounts which the nationalised industries contributed to rates, Poole's rateable value had only risen from £2592 in 1946 to £2700 in 1951, and it was little comfort to ratepayers to argue that more than three-quarters of the houses in Poole were rated at £18 or less. The members of the council were always extremely sensitive to criticism of any increase in rates, and it was beginning to look that quite a substantial increase of rates was inevitable the following April.

But, when the members of the Council heard that the County Council was considering increasing its rate demand on the council by 2/4d (12p) in the £, they were positively incensed. They were not the lone district councillors to be worried at the prospect. The Bridport Council wrote expressing its great concern, and Weymouth Council was said to be equally perturbed. The Poole Council compared the cost of education in Poole compared with the rest of the County and decided that the County Council was too profligate in its expenditure on education. Most of all, it considered that the County Council's system of paying for many of its capital projects out of one year's revenue, rather than by loan, was another cause of the County's projected increased demands.

Miss Llewellin, the Mayor, called a meeting of County Councillors representing the municipal boroughs of the County to discuss the question. The meeting was unanimous in asking for a meeting with the County Council to express its concern and to discuss ways in which the County's demands could be reduced.

It was then the turn of the Chairman and Vice-chairman of the County Council to become incensed. They considered that the holding of the meeting which the Dorset Non-County Boroughs had requested to discuss a confidential report of the County Council, was quite improper. The report had not then been before the meeting of the County Council, and it was an outrageous request that it should be discussed with outside bodies before it had been considered by the full County Council. They refused, point-blank, to receive the proposed deputation. They did add, however, that they would be willing to ask the County Finance Committee to consider any concrete proposals for economy which might be put to them.

Much of this controversy revolved round Councillor Lloyd-Allen who was not only a County Councillor, but the Vice-Chairman of the County Finance Committee. He had always taken the view that it would have been more equitable for the County Council to have spread the cost of its capital projects by paying for them by way of a loan, with repayments spread over a number of year, rather than by calling on the present ratepayers to pay immediately for development designed to benefit future residents.

It was, though, not an unusual quarrel between non-county boroughs and their county councils now that many of the powers of local councils had been transferred to the county councils, for the district councils were then having to collect more rates for the county council than for themselves. As a result of that particular quarrel Poole Council made a defiant gesture of making one 'concrete proposal' for economy. It suggested that, as building workers' summer working hours had then been reduced from 46 to 44 hours a week, the hours of work of County Hall staff should be brought into line by being increased from $38\frac{1}{2}$ hrs to 44!

But the more serious consequences were that Councillor Lloyd-Allen, whose thoughts on economy and how local government should be financed were far from those of the county council members, resigned from the County Council to concentrate on the affairs of the borough, and the Poole Council's thoughts were again turned to its ambition of attaining County Borough status.

Ealing Council had that year had promoted a Bill in Parliament, designed to give it County Borough Status, but the government had blocked its progress. Poole joined with it and eight of the other non-county boroughs which had earlier been recommended for County Borough status in petitioning the Minister of Housing & Local Government for him to submit an enabling Act to Parliament for them to be made county boroughs. Then, when that had failed, Poole, feeling it had a better case than most, petitioned the Minister on its own behalf. But the Government was not to be hurried. It would bring forward its own proposals, it was said, as soon as it was in a position to do so.

There was, though, the analagous problem of Poole's postal address. Lord de la Warr, the new Postmaster General, agreed to receive a deputation from the Council to consider Poole's postal address. The Council appointed three members of the Council, with the Town Clerk and the Chairman of the Society of Poole Men, to put its case, and they were received by Lord de la Warr with sympathy and understanding. He told them that he was most impressed by the case they had put forward. He said that he agreed that a town of the size and importance of Poole should be correctly designated in all postal matters.

The deputation returned to Poole certain that this time they had succeeded, and that it was time for Poole to get ready for all its districts at last to have a 'Poole' address. The difficulty which was foreseen was the fact that so many Poole roads had the same name. There were, for instance, four roads named Albert Road or Albert Avenue, and five named Harbour Hill or Harbour View Road; there were four 'Station Roads', three 'Kings Roads', and many more such examples. No less than 147 roads in the borough were affected. There was only a little opposition of householders to the many changes of road names, for many had already experienced difficulties in the duplication of names, and at the end of the exercise there were many new road names in Poole, such as Abbotsbury Road, Recreation Road, Hayden Road, Creech Road, Warwick Road, New Quay Road.

But, after all this bother, Poole Council's hopes were dashed again! In September the Town Clerk received a letter from the Post Office, saying that 'The Postmaster General had approached the problem with a strong desire to do what was practicable to remove the present postal difficulties. It could only be done through correspondence being dealt with at one sorting office, and none were large enough. He had considered hutments, but even then it would be inadequate and the expense not justified. He would review the position at frequent intervals and, when the Post Office could rebuild, he would discuss it again with the Council.'

Another disappointment to the Council was the Government's continuing ban on new industry coming to Poole. The local paper reflected the Council's irritation. 'The Government is stopping Poole's progress', it announced. But, with the Board of Trade continuing with its policy of granting permission for new industry on the basis of the unemployment situation in the area concerned, Poole had little grounds for appeal. Its average yearly unemployment since the end of the war had never been as much as 500 and, in 1951, had been only 356. This, no doubt, was because its existing industries were doing comparatively well. That year, Wallis Tin had taken back most of the workforce which it had laid off in 1951. Humphris Engineering in West Quay Road were working night shifts; Poole Pottery was at last allowed to produce decorated pottery; the Alder Road bakery was producing over 250,000 loaves a day; Arthur Butler & Co was employing 150 people in its brush factory in South Road; Bluebird Caravans was extending its works at Newtown, and British Drug Houses Co (BDH) which had built a factory on the mudlands of West Quay Road, was thriving.

But the greatest change in Poole industry that year was the coming into full production of the Generating Station. It had changed the sky-line of Poole with its two octagonal, 325 feet high, chimneys, but it was the unforeseen effect on the traffic travelling between Poole Old Town and Hamworthy which was most felt in Poole. The Generating Station's voracious appetite for coal which it consumed at the rate of 1000 tons a day, meant that colliers from Humberside were regularly passing through Poole Bridge, causing the bridge having to be opened much more frequently. The Poole Herald reported that, with the two level crossings at the top of the town being closed 100 times a day for an average time of three minutes, this amounted to the crossings being closed to traffic for 5 hours each day. Adding this to the fact Poole Bridge was then being closed to traffic between 12 and 20 times a day for a period of 15 minutes, it made 'Poole about as impregnable for road traffic as an ancient walled town'!

The Council had already considered what might be done about the problem. A year earlier it had persuaded the Railway Executive to install a mechanical system of opening and closing the railway gates, and it had discussed various alternatives to Poole Bridge for travel between the Old Town and Hamworthy, and had opted for a wider bridge, high enough to allow passage through it of all but the tallest ships. It had submitted its proposals to the Ministry, but it was more in hope than with any confidence that early action would be taken.

But for the rest of the year, it was mainly a case of planning for the future. That year, after completing its formal consultation with the Council, the County Council published the Development Plan for public consultation.

Most of the proposed developments were well known and accepted in the town. Some, such as the reclamation of the land at Turlin Moor by the Electricity Generating Board and the purchase of the 8 acres of land for the extension of Hamworthy Park, had already been agreed to be implemented by the Corporation, and the only two proposals which excited public interest were, curiously, two projects which had been agreed by the Council prior to the war.

The first of these was the proposal to reclaim 82 acres of mudland from Parkstone Bay between Poole Quay and Whitecliff. This proposal aroused more opposition than any other. It was a project which had first been agreed by the Council in 1928, but nothing had been done to bring it into effect. The proposal in the Development Plan was to use this new land fronting the harbour to provide a deep-water yacht basin, a swimming bath and bathing beaches and what was described as a 'subsidiary connection between the Old Town and Whitecliff', which the local newpaper interpreted as a new 'marine drive'. The main opposition to this proposal came from the Parkstone Yacht Club and its members who feared the effect which the proposed reclamation and yacht basin might have on the Club's facilities, but there were also objections to the scheme

Top: Arthur Butler & Co's advertisement from the Pageant programme.

Bottom: The Poole Generating Station, 1952.

A POOLE INDUSTRY WITH AN ANCIENT LINEAGE

More than one hundred years ago the trading fleets of Poole were braving the North Atlantic carrying on Poole's prosperous trade with Newfoundland. It was the golden era of Poole's commercial prosperity. Industry was flourishing. One of the important industries in Poole which shared in this boom was Brush-making. The works were situated in the High Street, near the Antelope Hotel, and over a hundred craftsmen were employed. Poole people used Poole-made Brushes. The ships in the harbour used these brushes and brooms, and they carried them as items of trade. In addition, horse-drawn wagons carried full loads to the principal towns of Dorset and Hampshire.

Before this time, possibly for hundreds of years, brushes had been made in Poole. What is more important, brushes have been made in the town continuously up to the present time. During the recent 30 years this Industry has changed from being an exclusively skilled craft to highly mechanised production with specialised high output machines, but still retaining the services of skilled craftsmen.

The full range of processes, including the preparation of materials, the shaping of the wood backs and the making of the brushes, are now carried out in modern factory premises in South Road, Poole. This factory is one of the most modern in the land and is classed, with respect to output, as one of the six largest in Great Britain. Brushes and brooms are shipped to all parts of the World.

This Factory, with a tradition of hundred of years of skilled craftsmanship, is owned by Arthur Butler Ltd., and is noted for the very high quality of Brushes and Brooms manufactured.

The famous brands Seagull, Turnpike and Signal are recognised throughout England as the hall marks indicating superior quality. These brushes are to be seen in the best Ironmongers and Stores and are purchased by those who appreciate how effective cleaning can be with really good brushes.

from local residents who feared that their view of the harbour might be affected, and some feared the effect on their roads of lorries which would be needed to transport the necessary filling to the site.

The other proposal which excited some public opposition was another pre-war resolution by the Council to reclaim an area, 100 yards wide and 1200 yards long from the harbour at Sandbanks to provide extra car parking space. Again, residents feared that the proposed car park would intrude on their view of the harbour and, they claimed, that to do this as a permanent feature when the car park would be used only for some four months a year, was unreasonable.

The Committees of the Council considered the representations which had been made against the Development Plan proposals. There were, altogether, 456 objections, most of them in regard to the reclamation of Parkstone Bay. As a result of its reconsideration of the proposals, it decided to reduce the area of reclamation retaining enough to provide a road link between the Old Town and Whitecliff.

There were no proposals in the plan for any extension of shopping in Poole. It was proposed that High Street should remain the principal shopping area of the town, with Ashley Road, Upper Parkstone, as the secondary area. In fact, coincidentally, the Board of Trade had that year completed its first survey of shopping facilities in the country. It reported that Britain had one shop per 89 persons, compared with one shop per 131 persons in the United States. Poole was reported to have 1686 shops and 283 'service trade establishments', and these facts led the Poole Herald to announce boldly that 'Poole had better shopping facilities than almost any other town of its size in the country'.

But there were lighter moments in Poole during 1952, even for members of the Council and its staff. It was the year when the brain-child of the Hon Mrs FitzGerald, who owned and operated the Fitz Club in Canford Cliffs, to hold a Poole pageant, came to fruition. Gwen Lally, 'the World's Pageant Master', who had been responsible for many pageants in various parts of the country, was commissioned to organise the event. H P Smith, the Poole historian, with the help of Miss Margaret Scott, an historical novelist of Poole, agreed to write the libretto. Mr B G Hillier was persuaded to become the business manager, and Miss Elizabeth Gifford produced the three ballets required for the production.

It was, therefore, an event devised and organised by the people of Poole and it captured the imagination and the enthusiastic support of the public. No less than 1500 people of Poole volunteered to take part in the pageant, either as 'mortals', 'neriads', 'fisher girls', 'villagers', 'tritons' or 'ladies and gentlemen of distinction'. John Valentine of the Society of Poole Men even gave up shaving so that he could appear as Edward, Prince of Wales (and then liked the effect which his newly grown beard gave him, and kept it for the rest of his life!). Miss Llewellin and her brother W W Llewellin became deeply involved and took leading parts

Top: Gwen Lally, the World's Pageant Master.

Bottom: Poole Pageant 1952.

in the production, as did many other Councillors and officers of the Council, headed by Wilson Kenyon, the Town Clerk, and his wife.

For such a universally supported event, the Council readily agreed to the Seldown end of Poole Park being enclosed and an adjoining area of the lake roped off for the Pageant. Stands were erected there to hold up to 2000 spectators, advertising banners were allowed to be erected over the entrances to the park and, unprecedentedly, the Council agreed to lend its robes and regalia for use in some of the episodes of the pageant.

The pageant itself was composed of nine episodes of Poole's history, beginning with the Roman invasion of Hamworthy in AD 44, and ending with the opening of Poole Park by the Prince of Wales in 1890, all linked together by 'Old Harry', who was supposed to have witnessed all of Poole's history from his vantage at the entrance to the harbour, and who spoke with the authentic Dorset speech of Ralph Wightman of the BBC as 'narrator' on the first night and G W Skeggs on other nights. The performance began with Old Harry's prologue, after a fanfare of Trumpeters, and 'a flush of Sunset brought up on Old Harry' to a peal of Thunder, and then an Introductory Greeting from Old Harry:

Good neighbours all and my very good friends,
I bid 'ee a hearty good day,
Vor O've a-come from they wave-beat Chalk Stacks
Out yonder to west of Poole Bay.

To join in this wunnerful Pay-geant
And to tell 'ee what you'm gwain to zee
And to hear about fair lovely POLA,
Vor Queen of the coast she be.

Zo Zit 'ee zelves down and tend to our show,
While the story of POLA we trace
Droo all the long years of her history
To this present Year of Grace.

On the first night on 4 August, the stand was full and included 20 Mayors of nearby towns and, although Poole's usual bad luck with weather delayed the start of the proceedings for some time, the worst fears of a power cut with the Electricity Board's then common 'power shedding' programme did not happen that night. It was quite late that night, therefore, when Ralph Wightman finally gave 'Old Harry's Farewell':

'Kind vriends our story be now vinished,
Zo I'll bid 'ee very good day,
And now that this pay-geant be ended,
I'll went my way back to Poole Bay,
Where I'll stand, as of old, POLA's guardian,
Keeping watch as in faith I must,
Till my old eyes grow dim with peeren,
And my figure do crumble to dust.'

INDEX